PRESENTED TO

_____

"For He, Himself has said,
I will never leave you nor forsake you.
So we may boldly say:
The Lord is my helper;
I will not fear…"
Hebrews 13:5-6

FROM:

_____

God's GPS

He knows where you are

Gail Gammill

Gail Gammill
Joshua 1:9

Copyright © 2019 Gail Gammill

All rights reserved. This book is protected under the Copyright Act of 1976 of the United States of America. This publication may not be reproduced, distributed, or transmitted in any form or stored in a database or retrieval system for commercial gain or profit without the written permission of the author. Short quotations or page copying is permitted and encouraged for personal or group study. Permission will be granted upon request.

Unless otherwise noted, all Scripture is taken from The Holy Bible, New King James Version. Copyright © 1982 by Thomas Nelson, Inc. Used by permission. All rights reserved.

Scripture quotations marked AMP are taken from the Amplified Bible, Copyright © 1954, 1958, 1962, 1964, 1965, 1987 by The Lockman Foundation. Used by permission.

Several Scripture passages have been paraphrased in the author's own words.

Cover design by Jacee Gammill
Interior design by Allison Fowler

Publishing Services provided by:
M&N Marketing Group

Printed in the United States of America
For Worldwide Distribution
Library of Congress Control Number: 2019939444
ISBN-13: 978-1-7336518-0-6

First Edition: February 2019
Second Edition: September 2019

To order your copy of God's GPS
Email: info@cathedraloflife.org

FOREWORD

I believe miracles happen all around us everyday! Our God is a miracle working God! So often we get so busy in our daily lives that we miss the little expressions of God's love and kindness toward us. While we long to see the "supernatural" and the "unusual," we fail to appreciate the common and the ordinary. Acts 19:11, Amplified Version, says that "God did unusual and extraordinary miracles by the hands of Paul." This verse tells me that our God does the extraordinary, but it also leads me to believe He is actively involved in even ordinary Divine interventions of life. It is evident that God clearly cares about even the little things.

My mother, the author of this book taught me to expect God to show up in our lives every day. She also taught me to trust God for everything with a childlike faith. When I was six years old, we had just moved to a new city. I told my mother I was so sad because I didn't have any friends. She said, "Let's pray. Ask God to send you a new friend." While kneeling in prayer, there was a knock at our front door. When we opened the door, a lady and her son were standing on our front porch. She asked if there were any children in this house. Her husband was a minister and her son was looking for a playmate. No way was that a coincidence. I cannot tell you how that experience built up my faith to believe God for anything.

This book is filled with amazing miracle stories of hope and faith. You will read stories of both the ordinary and the extraordinary! Each chapter is filled with insights, principles, and promises that will cause you to long for encounters with God too, just like our family has experienced. You will certainly laugh and maybe even cry as you read these miraculous testimonies. May God open your eyes to see His signs and wonders everyday!

Dr. M. Dana Gammill
Cathedral of Life
Senior Pastor

DEDICATION

To my parents, Frank and Christine Mefford and my siblings... Donna, Harvey, Yvonne, Dale, Mary, and Cheryl who were my constant companions in my growing up years;

To my husband, Herschel and our family which is our greatest treasure:
    Children: Dana and Nan, Deana,
    Grandchildren: Michael and Jacee,
        Allison and Hunter, Blake,
and our little Jordan and Grace, who we will meet for the first time in Heaven;
    Great-grandchildren: Isabella, Elizabeth,
        Issac and Levi;

To my forever family of lifetime friends who have faithfully stood with our family through the years; and to every reader who has longed for a personal relationship with God;

And most of all, I dedicate this book...
To God who knew me first, who knows me best, and loves me most.

ACKNOWLEDGEMENTS

I extend a special thank you:

To Hunter and Allison Fowler for teaching me to use an iPad, copying the manuscript on their flash drive and computer, and printing and formatting my first hard copy;

To Jacee Gammill for designing the cover;

To my advisors, Monica Nagy and llke Peh, and especially John Woolf, who was the first person to proofread and edit the manuscript;

To my brothers, Harvey and Dale, and my sister Mary, who sat and read every word in my final draft, giving me input and inspiring me with their reactions as they reminisced the faithfulness of God in every chapter.;

To every person who encouraged me to put into print the miracles I have experienced throughout my lifetime, and especially, my sister, Donna, who asked me to promise to write my story someday;

To Paul and Leanne Frye who generously helped make the publishing of this book possible. They will forever become an important part of anything it accomplishes;

I will be eternally grateful for all of the love and support. Thank you for helping me present the message of this book:

God's GPS
He Knows Where You Are

PREFACE

This has to be one of the most significant times to be alive in the history of the world. This present generation will see things come to pass like no other has witnessed. We sit in our living rooms and watch the chaos while it is happening around the globe. Can you imagine the aerial vision of our Father God from His throne in Heaven? He has a peripheral view of the past, the present, and the future all at the same time. He said, "Heaven is my throne and earth is my footstool," Isaiah 66:1.

There is no place you can go from His presence. The Bible makes it clear in Psalm 139:8-10, "If I ascend into heaven, You are there; If I make my bed in hell, behold, You are there. If I take the wings of the morning, And dwell in the uttermost parts of the sea, Even there Your hand shall lead me, And Your right hand shall hold me."

God's Global Positioning System has a universal, navigational surveillance facility that transcends all time and space. His unlimited reception signals make even the most sophisticated satellites fade in comparison. The Bible declares in Psalm 102:19,... "From Heaven the Lord viewed the earth."..."He hangs the earth on nothing," Job 26:7..."All things were created through Him and for Him. And He is before all things, and in Him all things consist," Colossians 1:16,17. "For in Him we live and move and have our being," Acts 17:28. There is no place God is not. In the middle of it all, God is there!

Have you wondered how big is God? "Who has measured the waters in the hollow of His hand, Measured heaven with a span, And has calculated the dust of the earth in a measure? Weighed the mountains in scales, And the hills in a balance? Isaiah 40:12." I wish it were possible to convey His majesty. He spoke... and by His Words the world came into existence.

My son painted a word portrait of God:
He is the Creator and the first born of all Creation.
He is the first... and the last.
He is the beginning... and the end.
He is the provider... and the provision.
He is the architect... and the plan.
He is the singer... and the song.
He is the messenger... and the message.
He is the warrior... and the weapon.
He is the peacemaker... and the peace.
He is the builder... and the tool.
He is the bread maker... and the Bread.
He is the choreographer ... and the dance.

Are you getting the picture?

In Him is "everything" we will ever need. God introduces Himself as, *"I Am that I Am."* Before time began, He was, He is, and will always be... All I know is that He has always been there for me. His presence is as high as the heavens and as deep as the ocean. His love has no boundaries. He loves us with an unending, everlasting love.

How do you describe the greatness of God? The word, amazing, appears repeatedly on the pages of this book. It means to cause great surprise or wonder, startlingly impressive, and astonishing! The universe that God created has been defined as: "All of space and time and their contents, including planets, stars, galaxies, and all other forms of matter and energy." His excellence is more than my mind can conceive. His Holy Spirit fills the universe. I am in awe!!!

In this book, I will attempt to share with you that ... "GOD'S GPS KNOWS WHERE YOU ARE!"

THE CONTENTS
Foreword
Preface

The Introduction	1
The Times and Seasons	5
The Sunflower	11
The Storm	15
The Design	19
The Rose	25
The Dream	29
The Challenge	35
The Lion	43
The Prom-ise Dress	47
The Wish	53
The Christmas Present	57
The Spider	61
The July Fourth Weekend	67
The Surprise	71
The Red Dress	75
The Message	79
The Cross and the Switchblade	83
The Divine Love Connection	93
The Unlimited Provision	99
The Miracle on 38th Street	105

The Gammill House	111
The Inn	117
The Robin	123
The Wake-Up Call	129
The Assignment	135
The Last Mile	141
The Sign	151
The Angelic Encounters	157
The Eagle	165
The Abundant Life	169
The Big Picture	175
The Lily of the Valley	183
The Tornado	187
The Wedding	191
The Elephant Earring	195
The Lost and Found Department	201
The Seed	207
The Questions	215
The Answers	221
The Overcomer	227
The Stress Factor	235
The Restoration Process	243
The Celebration of Life	251
The Presence of God	259
The Epilogue	265

Alphabetized Contents
My Prayer for You
About the Author

THE INTRODUCTION

For years, I was asked, "When are you going to write a book? My answer was always, "Someday." Typically, many times someday ends up in a pile of good intentions. It eventually gets discarded, or placed in the basement with the rest of the clutter I don't want to deal with at the moment. Years ago, I remember my son asking me to buy a blue suede jacket that was on sale. I said, "Maybe, someday." Wrong answer. He exclaimed, "Someday?" It was thought provoking because it could be sold and gone tomorrow.

One day we realize some of the things we thought were so important today may not matter. If we continue waiting for someday, it is possible for precious moments of opportunity to evaporate into that mystical place called, "Never." By the way, I returned to the store that day. The suede jacket was reduced again and I bought it for thirteen dollars.

While I was standing in line to make a purchase in a book store, I noticed a book titled: *"Don't Throw Away Tomorrow."* I commented, "I think I'll write a book entitled: *"Don't Throw Away Today."* A lady asked if I was an author. I replied, "Not yet." She told me to follow my dream and someday she will say, "I met the author."

One day I made a decision. I wrote at the top of my daily *"To Do List":* 1. Don't throw away today. Today, I will make my dream come true. Today, I will begin writing and watch the stories of God's supernatural intervention unfold from the pages of my life. I typed these words: ... **"God's GPS ... He knows Where You Are."** —By Gail Gammill

This book is not intended to be an autobiography. *The stories may not appear in the order they happened.* They are not about me. *They are incredible events of personal life changing experiences of God's love and faithfulness through the years.* My ultimate purpose in putting these phenomenal memoirs into print is to give glory to God.

I pray that the message presented in this book, *"God Knows Where You Are"* will challenge every reader to develop an even greater awareness of His ever-abiding presence; that God's GPS will lead those who desire a personal encounter with Him into a dimension of intimacy and relationship with Jesus Christ; that faith, hope, and courage will be increased and instilled into every heart; and that it will inspire others to share their own testimony of the miracles they have witnessed.

God shows up in astounding ways. His greatness is beyond comprehension. The Bible is the most fascinating book ever written. It records historical accounts which are so spectacular, our skeptical society views it as another fantasy in a modern day movie. Take the story of *"The Exodus,"* for example; Moses appears on the scene like a Super Hero rescuing his people from four hundred years of slavery. His story is unbelievable.

The Pharaoh made a decree that all Hebrew male babies under the age of two had to be put to death. When Moses was born, his mother hid him in the weeds beside the water where a princess came to bathe. He ended up being rescued by the Pharaoh's daughter and grew up in the Palace. His own mother became his nursemaid.

When the Pharaoh denied his request to let his people go, Moses became God's agent to set them free. The shortest distance to the Promised Land was across the Red Sea. The water literally rolled up like a scroll allowing them to walk across on dry land. Ironically, the Egyptian armies pursuing them were drowned in the exact same spot.

God has been there through the eons of time. He arrives in the story of every man, woman, boy, and girl. His love reaches into every generation, every nation, and every tribe. Each of us have a Divine appointment with destiny.

Moses was born to deliver the children of Israel from bondage. He wasn't perfect. His bitterness toward injustice turned into hatred. He lost his temper and murdered an Egyptian man who was persecuting an Israelite. Moses acknowledged his failure and didn't allow it to prevent him from fulfilling his destiny.

I have a question for you. Why were *you* born? Do you know why God chose for you to be here? Who and what is influencing the direction your life is heading? Don't wait for *"someday."* When you make room for God's plans in your daily routine, He will direct your path.

Come with me through the pages of this journey we call, "life." Watch God's GPS appear in every struggle with a plan to meet every need. In this book you will read story after story of modern day miracles, signs, and wonders. These extraordinary, fascinating adventures will leave you in awe of His ever-abiding presence.

I write in conversational tones. Go get a cup of coffee and sit down in your favorite chair, while I share with you the amazing reality that God is beyond awesome!
        He Knows Where You Are!

CHAPTER ONE

THE TIMES AND SEASONS

I enjoy experiencing the change of each season. I love seeing the very first signs of springtime, with the first daffodil peeking up through the soil, and red-winged black birds announcing that winter is almost over... And then, surprise! I wake up one morning and it is a winter wonderland again. The ground is covered in a blanket of snow, sparkling like diamonds in the sunlight. Whether it is sitting in front of a fireplace on a snowy day, or wearing a warm coat with my snow boots making footprints in the snow... I love winter. *me too!*

Finally, the robins are back. Soft, pastel shades of blossoms begin to bloom. New life appears when the leaves return to the trees and the ground is covered with green grass growing in the warmth of the sunshine. It's fun wearing sandals or going barefoot, walking in the rain showers, and seeing raindrops dancing in the street. But one day, the chill is back in the air and the leaves begin turning into the bright colors of red, gold, and orange. The only thing in life that doesn't change is the fact that God never changes. There never has been and never will be anyone like Him. God is, and will always be the same; yesterday, today, and forever.

Each season in life is accompanied with unique difficulties. Whether it is blizzards, hurricanes, tornados, or floods, the storms in life come and go. The seasons reflect the changing stages of our life. My son wrote in his newspaper column, "Just as an artist uses both dark and light colors and with the stroke of a brush blends them into a painting creating a work of art, so are the 'Days of our Lives.' Each of us live out our own soap opera because life is made up of bright, happy times and dark, sad times. Each phase of life is a part of ….the rest of the story."

One decision, one phone call, one doctor's report, one unexpected incident, can send you spiraling into a season of either joy or despair. The Bible says in Ecclesiastes 3:1, "To everything there is a season, A time for every purpose under heaven." Looking back over my life, I can see the GPS of Divine Providence guiding every step, healing every hurt, and giving me courage and strength for each day. There are always new opportunities for growth and development. We go from infancy to childhood, from being a teenager to a young adult, to the responsibilities that go along with maturity. Each season takes us on a journey filled with choices that are determining our destiny.

7

Some seasons of life can seem so mundane, like performing the task of washing the same dishes after each meal or folding the same towels in the laundry room.

In one of those "life is so daily moments" I was standing at the kitchen sink remembering exciting experiences when I was a teenager witnessing to teen gangs and drug addicts in New York City. But now, every day was filled with caring for my toddler and five year old. I decided to take them with me and visit everyone in my neighborhood and tell them about the Lord Jesus. At the first house, Deana started crying and Dana took off on the tricycle sitting on my next door neighbor's front porch. I gave up on the idea.

I went back to my kitchen to finish the dishes and my doorbell rang. Standing at the door was an old man. He was obviously inebriated. The words of that grand hymn, *"The Old Rugged Cross,"* were blaring from my record player. I closed and locked the door, but he kept standing there, weeping.

I called a young man who was on break from Bible College. When he arrived, I unlocked the church next door. The man staggered down the aisle and knelt before the open Bible lying on the altar. He said his mother used to sing that song to him. He told us the story of how he had wasted years of his life. He obviously came to ask for money, but received something money can't buy. He received forgiveness. God saw the desire of my heart and brought someone in need right to my front door. An ordinary day became an exciting life-changing, Divine appointment with destiny. Every season is filled with purpose.

Each day begins a new story. One time I was in excruciating pain because of some complications following a surgery. My husband walked into the room. He opened his Bible and read, "And it came to pass." I expected a great faith-building promise. He just smiled and said, "This too shall pass. Let's pray." One day, life was back to normal. The pain was gone and I hardly remembered it happened. Sometimes, our best of times and worst of times happen at the same time. "I trust in You, O Lord, I say, You are my God; My times are in Your hand," Psalm 31:14-15.

Look for the purpose and reason for the season. Every impossibility will present you with a new opportunity *"to believe."* The obstacles in each step of your journey provide possibilities to become triumphant. When you are in the middle of a crisis, it can feel like life will never be the same again. Let hope emerge! God will never leave you. Like the man God's GPS sent to my door years ago, even failure is not final unless you refuse to try again. A new season and a new day is always on the way. He knows where you are.

… I thought I ended this chapter months ago. It is the middle of another sleepless night. I decided I should share early in the book why my husband is conspicuously missing in some of the stories. Herschel has been suffering for several years from a progressive mental deterioration of his brain. He was diagnosed with Frontotemporal Dementia. As the level of care has increased, we have exhausted our strength and finances. I am feeling the weight of the accumulated stress that is taking its toll on every member of my family.

Herschel rarely recognizes us. The sadness I see in my children's eyes is almost more than I can bear. Only God can bring relief to the pain in our hearts. My *feelings* would like for me to believe, *"I am at the end of my resources. I spent the money I was going to use to publish this book to hire more help. Perhaps, these words were never written for anyone, but me."* So tonight, I remind myself to rest on the pillow of God's promises. "Let the weak say, I am strong."

The timing for this book being written graphically illustrates God's faithfulness in every story. Our coping mechanisms reveal when we are carrying weight God never designed for us to carry. He not only gives us strength, He "is" our strength. I will dismiss my feelings and tell my faith to arise. Jesus stated in 2 Corinthians 12:9, "...My grace is sufficient for you, for My strength is made perfect in weakness."

My son, Dana said, "We can either *go* through this season, or *grow* through this season." As we trust in God, our faith reaches a new level of spiritual maturity. As we wait in His presence our strength is renewed. I will be ready to face tomorrow. God is my light in the darkness. I will lie down and sleep in His peace. When I wake up, He will still be there. He knows where I am.

I have to add another paragraph. It is Sunday. I just wrote the previous statements at four o'clock this morning. At the end of our morning church service, someone approached me and said that he and his wife would like to finance the publishing of my book. He is a graphic arts designer and can advise me in making it happen. I was speechless. I never cease to be amazed at the greatness of God and His intervention in my life.

Recently, after leaving my husband in The Inn at Belden Village Memory Care facility I sat in my car and asked, "God, do you care?" The answer is found in 1 Peter 5:7, "... casting all your care upon Him, *for He cares for you.*" The question is not, "Does God care? The question is, "Do you trust Him?" His peace arrives when you leave your worries and anxieties with Him. Someone reading this book may be experiencing a similar crisis. Be encouraged. In every season, God is still God... of course, He cares. You are never alone. He knows where you are.

CHAPTER TWO
THE SUNFLOWER

Most of the time, I am a morning person. I usually wake up refreshed with a feeling of excitement about another new day. Every day is a day the Lord has made and that truth, all by itself, is a reason to rejoice. Don't waste today. My mother painted and framed this quote for me: "Today well lived makes every yesterday a dream of happiness and every tomorrow a vision of hope." I passed it on to my children, my grandchildren, and now I will begin sharing this powerful truth with my great-grandchildren.

At night, God turns the light out and leaves the moon for a nightlight. In the morning, He sends the sunshine to wake us up so that we won't miss anything He has planned for us. For years, in warm weather I loved to take an early walk with God and watch the sun come up. The sky was painted with pale shades of pink. It was inspiring seeing the rays of light shining through the trees. While my family was sleeping, I slipped outside and talked to God about my day. In the quietness of the morning, the only noises are the sounds of nature. With less distractions, it is easy to become more aware of the presence of our Creator and hear His voice more clearly.

Unfortunately, life isn't all rainbows and roses. It takes rain to make a rainbow, and even the most beautiful, fragrant roses have their thorns. Life is like a roller coaster. It has its ups and downs, good times and bad times. When our grandson, Michael was a little guy, he overheard us talking about a frustrating situation and commented, "Well, this is how life lives."

His words were never forgotten and quoted often in our family through the years. Difficult times and seasons are a part of life. It is easy to become overwhelmed with all of the "what if's" and "if only's." We overcome moments of uncertainty, as we face each day with the certainty that we are not alone. God is always there...

During a season, when it seemed like everything that could go wrong was happening all at the same time, I walked outside on my front porch in the middle of the night. I looked up at the moon and stars. Why does everything seem so much worse at night? Somewhere, there is a place called Heaven that has no need for the sun or the moon. God, Himself, illuminates the entire atmosphere! Can you imagine a place where there is "no more" darkness and "no more" sorrow?

The Bible says in Psalm 30:5 that ..."Weeping may endure for a night, But joy comes in the morning." I asked, "God, are You here? I grew up on the corner of 802 South C Street in Arkansas City, Kansas. Do You know where I live? I don't live in Kansas anymore. I live in Ohio now. Do You know my address?"

The next morning after my walk, I stopped to pull weeds and remove the dead stems in my flower garden beside my front porch. I noticed a little plant I hadn't seen. I decided to leave it alone. It grew rapidly and soon, it had a bloom. When the bud opened up, much to my surprise I discovered it was a sunflower. I was amazed!

The Sunflower is the Kansas State Flower. God's GPS had to have guided that little seed to my garden. They grow wild in the fields. A sunflower re-seeds itself, multiplies, and comes back every year. There was only one. It only bloomed that season. It never came back... It didn't have to return. God put it there to tell me, "I know your address. I know where you live."

Faith in God bypassed my circumstances and my feelings. It is connected to the assurance that He is there. When His presence invades any area of our life, darkness and sadness have to flee. Depression has to go. It has no choice. Joy is on the way. God shows up in unusual and unexpected places.

1 John 1:5 declares that… "God is light and in Him is no darkness at all." It is recorded in Exodus 34:29, that after God met with Moses on Mount Sinai to give him the Ten Commandments, the brightness of his countenance became so intense a veil had to be placed over his face for the people to even look upon him.

Read the entire chapter of Psalm 27. It starts out in the first verse saying, "The Lord is my *light* and my salvation. Whom shall I fear? The Lord is the strength of my life, Of whom shall I be afraid?" The eighth verse says, "When You said, "Seek My face," 'My heart said to You,' "Your face, Lord I will seek." The final verse says, "Wait on the Lord. Be of good courage. And He shall strengthen your heart; wait I say on the Lord."

Isaiah 60:1 says, "Arise, shine; for Your light has come and the glory of the Lord is risen upon you." Look for Him today. He can even speak through a sunflower. God has unique ways to reveal Himself to you. He knows where you are.

CHAPTER THREE
THE STORM

When my children were young, we went on a trip to South Carolina for a Children's Crusade. I had to drive late into the night to arrive home on time for school the following morning. We were in the middle of a ferocious storm. It was raining so hard I could barely see the road. I had limited visibility in every direction. There wasn't any place to stop and turn around. It was as dangerous to try to pull off the road as it was to keep going. I didn't even know if I was in the right lane. There was no light except split second moments of lightning flashing across the sky with crashing sounds of thunder.

The darkness was overwhelming. I had no idea if we were still headed in the right direction. GPS and cell phones didn't exist back then. There was no way to call for help. I was on a County Road feeling like I was in the middle of nowhere. It was a blessing that there were no other cars on the road. With almost zero visibility, that would have been even more unsafe. My little daughter was afraid. She asked, "Mommy, are we lost? Do you know where we are?" I said, "God knows!"

The children had no idea how scared I was feeling, but God did! The only thing I could think about was the name of Jesus. My son was in the back seat singing, *"He's got the whole world in His hands."* He kept repeating the words of that song until they became a reality. God is here right now holding our car in his hands! We sang every verse over and over and made up verses of our own. God didn't just have the little babies, our brother and sister, and our mama and daddy in his hands. He was even holding "the wind and the rain" and we were in a safe place.

As we sang, the heaviness I felt in my chest began to disappear. The same peace of God that filled the disciple's boat in that terrible storm on the Sea of Galilee permeated the atmosphere. Fear vanished. Suddenly, I knew our exact location. We were in the hands of the Lord. God had it all in control. We couldn't be more safe!

Nothing had changed. The circumstances were the same. The rain was still pounding the windshield. The road was still slippery. It was difficult to keep the car from skimming like a hydroplane. The lightning was still flashing and the thunder was still roaring, but we were laughing and singing. The only thing we ran into was the name of the Lord. The Bible says in Proverbs 18:10, "The name of the Lord is a strong tower; The righteous run into it and are safe."

Guess what? God's GPS showed up. A big tractor trailer truck with bright lights came from behind us. The driver went around our car and stayed close enough for me to follow his tail lights. Every time he turned, I turned. Finally, the rain became a sprinkle. Lights began to show up in the distance. When we arrived, there were road signs to the highway that would lead us the rest of the way. The truck driver flashed his lights and waved as we headed toward home.

I am so thankful that in crisis situations, when it is impossible to call 911 or reach the AAA emergency road service, God is there. The password is the name of Jesus. Psalm 50:15 says, "Call upon Me in the day of trouble; I will deliver you and you shall glorify Me." We watched God keep His promise. It was a life-changing, faith-building, experience we would never forget. God's GPS knew our exact location. He miraculously sent the help we needed to protect and keep us safe. Put your trust in Him. God knows where you are.

"*Be still and know that I am God.*"
   -Psalm 46:10

You are here on purpose.
"This moment in time will only happen once,
so make your 'once upon a time'
worth happening."
   -Dana Gammill

CHAPTER FOUR
THE DESIGN

If there is a design, there has to be a designer. I read a story about an atheist who was trying to convince a Christian that God doesn't exist. He asked, "Why do you believe in God?" As they walked along the road, they noticed a little turtle sitting on top of a fence post. He answered his own question when he said, "Someone had to have put it there."

The whole story of creation begins with the first four words in the first book of the Bible; "In the beginning, God"... There is no attempt to prove His existence. He states the facts. Period! There is no debate. God is! As magnificent as it is, when God "designed" this indescribable universe, He simply spoke it into existence.

Genesis, chapter one states, "In the beginning God created the heavens and the earth. The earth was without form, and void; and darkness was on the face of the deep." He spoke, "Let there be light," and there was light! He separated the waters and the dry land appeared. He designed the plant and animal kingdoms, and the complex solar system with perfect balance. Scientists say that the Earth travels around the Sun at a rate of eighteen miles a second. If it had been six miles or forty miles, it would have been too far or too close for any form of life to exist. The detail is indescribable!

We existed in the mind of God even before the foundation of the world. As if He were designing the nursery...God looked through the ages and knew our exact birthdate and time of arrival. He designed and spoke into place everything we would ever need with precise symmetry... From the majestic mountains, to the depth of the oceans; from the creatures of the sea, to the exotic animals we visit and see at the zoo; from the fragrance of the thousands of species of plants and flowers, to the amazing vegetables and fruits in every color of the rainbow waiting for us to plant or purchase in the produce market ... "It's a Wonderful World!"

When God said, "Let us make man in our image," He scooped up the dust and fashioned the first man, Adam, with His own hands. He breathed into his nostrils the breath of life and man became a living being. So that he wouldn't be alone, God performed the first surgery. He caused Adam to fall into a deep sleep, removed one of his ribs and formed a woman to stand by his side. He placed within them the ability to birth and form a family. That is beyond amazing!

The anatomy of man cannot be replicated. The human brain exceeds the complex capabilities of our modern innovative computer technology. The physiological structure God created and designed with its organic, circulatory, and sewer system is unsurpassed. The human body has as an ability beyond our wildest imagination.

My husband tells an incredible story about his relatives whose car was tragically overturned in an accident. His cousin, who had been thrown from the car, rushed over and literally lifted it off of his uncle, who was crushed beneath. It was humanly impossible. The adrenaline that shot into his bloodstream gave him strength and power beyond his natural ability.

This is a vivid picture of what God does for us. He placed within us the ability to rise above every difficulty; the strength to face impossibilities; the determination to never give up; the courage to change the status quo; the faith to believe; the capacity to love and be loved. God wants us to live, laugh, and enjoy everything He designed.

After all I have attempted to describe about the design of this awesome universe, the greatest aspect of creation is the designer, Himself! The greatest attribute of God is not His omnipotence, omniscience, or omnipresence; it is not that He is all powerful or all knowing; it is not what He has done, or what He is capable of doing. It is "who" He is! God doesn't only love unconditionally with an everlasting love... God "is" love. God is good!

He desires to have relationship with you. It isn't enough to know *about* God. You can know Him personally. To say, "I only believe in what I see," is being intellectually dishonest. You can't see pain, but no one would deny its existence. You can't see the wind, but you can feel its force. You don't have to understand. All you have to do is believe. An unbeliever asked my son, "What if the Bible isn't true?" He answered with a question, "What if it is true? I have everything to gain and nothing to lose." ...What would you have to lose?

One by one, we enter into this time/space world. It seems like we blink our eyes and twenty years have passed. On my fiftieth birthday, I dressed up in my best black suit and high heels. Deana asked, "Where are you going so early in the morning?" I answered, "I'm going to the church. I have an appointment with God." I wanted to make sure I was still on target with His master design for my life. I opened my Bible to the book of Esther and read the whole book.

Esther was an orphan who had been raised by her uncle. She was secretly a Jew. Through a series of events, she was chosen to be the queen. An evil plot with a decree went forth that all Jews were to be killed. Queen Esther knew she was sovereignly born on purpose… "for such a time as this." God used her to save an entire nation. He doesn't require our ability. He asks for our availability. There is purpose in each day that gives meaning to life. Cherish the gift of the present. Pursue your purpose and access your potential.

God doesn't do anything by chance. He arranges specific Divine appointments. I was standing in line to make a purchase when a lady shoved me and pushed her shopping cart to the next cashier. As I was walking to my car, I thought, "I hope she gets where she is going on time." I was shocked when I felt an urgency to pray for her. "Now!" Unfortunately, we can't purchase time and we are only allotted a certain amount. I wondered if she realizes she was created for eternity. Someday her time on earth will run out. I looked for her but she was nowhere in sight. I prayed for God to send someone to speak into her life.

God *designed* each of us to make a difference for those in "our world." We have no promise of tomorrow. We are here on purpose, for a purpose. Would we live life differently if we understood we are here on assignment and will one day give an account to God? Would it change the items on our list of priorities today? Are you willing to make this commitment and say, "I'll go. Here am I, Lord, send me?" He knows where you are!

Give someone a rose today.

A rose is a message
that doesn't have to say a word,
like a rainbow that appears
silently saying, "The storm is over."

CHAPTER FIVE
THE ROSE

One night in a dream, I saw the face of a cashier who frequently bagged my food at the grocery store. She was crying. I don't dream often so I took it seriously. Out of nowhere these words entered my mind: A rose is a message that doesn't have to say a word, like a rainbow that appears silently saying, "The storm is over." While praying for her, I felt impressed to purchase a dozen red roses, present them to her, and tell her that God loves her. The next morning, I arrived at the store as soon as it opened. I walked to her cash register and placed the roses on the counter. She leaned down and smelled the roses.

While she was ringing them up she said, "No one has ever given me flowers." I said, "These are for you!" She looked shocked. I told her about the dream and explained that these are a gift to you from God. He wants you to know that He loves you. Tears started streaming down her cheeks. She told me that in the last month, some people in her family died. She stated that she was not handling it well because she didn't even know if there is a

God or a Heaven. I explained that God not only exists, He loves you. He wants you to know that Heaven is a real place where roses bloom with the freshness of never ending springtimes. I looked at her name tag. God knew her name even though she didn't know Him. He had seen every tear.

Can you believe God, Himself, ordered roses for her! The Scripture refers to Jesus as, *'The Rose of Sharon.'* At His crucifixion, He was mocked and a crown of thorns was placed on His head. No wonder the rose is such a powerful symbol of love. I think the thorns were placed on its stem to remind us of His suffering. "For God so loved the world, that He gave His only begotten Son, that *whosoever* believes in Him should not perish, but have everlasting life," John 3:16. KJV

Guess what! When you accept the gift of God's Son into your heart, you become His Rose. You receive His beauty, His fragrance, and His nature that touches and changes our world. Gloria told the other cashiers about her roses. When I was in the store, I had opportunities to pray with them.

Whether anyone ever sends you roses, remember that God had you in mind when He spoke the first petal into existence... In the beginning, He ordered all the roses that will ever exist for the whole world to enjoy. A red rose has a language of its own. It can say, "I love you," without making a sound. Take time to visit florists and gardens and enjoy the fragrance. Roses are personal gifts from our loving Heavenly Father. Spending time in His presence can turn any day into Valentine's Day.

Roses are found in every color and each variety, like each of us, is unique. Wild roses bring color to the countryside in the summertime. Roses grace the bridal bouquet, decorate our flower gardens, and the meals on our tables. Roses are sent to hospitals and funerals to bring messages of love and comfort. How fun it is to be a part of God's plan. I believe God gave me a dream to let me see someone who was hurting. Her tears touched my heart. God knew that He could use me to send a message from Him because I cared.

Recently, I was near the same grocery store where I shopped before we moved across town, thirteen years ago. I decided to stop and buy groceries. The cashier in the next aisle recognized me. I was surprised she remembered. She said that all of the other clerks no longer worked there. We were so happy to see each other.

One deed of kindness, one act of obedience can make a difference that will not be forgotten. Take time to care every day. God's GPS will either send someone to you or send you on an unexpected adventure. God may have a Divine appointment for you today.

Don't miss your moment. God speaks sometimes through Divine intuition. Early one morning God spoke to my daughter-in-law, Nan, to cancel her appointments and accompany the children on a school excursion to a lake. She saw a little girl jump into the water, but didn't come back up. No one else saw it happen. She didn't know how to swim. Instantly, Nan dived in and got her back on the shore. Because she recognized and obeyed the voice of God, she was able to save a little girl's life.

I had the privilege of driving my grandchildren to school in the mornings. While en-route, we took turns praying. Michael was nine years old. One morning, he stretched his hand toward a house as we drove by and began praying, "Father, in the name of Jesus, I come against the spirit of division that is coming against that family. Let Your peace fill that house." I asked, "Michael, do you know these people?" He answered," No, but God does." God is so awesome!!!

Oh, that we could always be that sensitive to the voice and heart of God! Are you so aware of the needs of others that when you drive past where they live you are moved with compassion?

I want to remind someone that Your prayers have come before the throne of God. He has seen every tear. He has not forgotten you. He knows your name. He loves you and He knows where you are.

CHAPTER SIX
THE DREAM

There are many references in the Bible of God speaking to people through dreams and visions. They occur in both the Old and New Testaments. They were always given for specific purposes to warn, give instruction, or reveal a future event. Dreams from God can be life changing. In the Old Testament, God gave a boy named Joseph three dreams. In the dreams, his older brothers had to bow down to him. When his brothers were told about the dream they became angry and plotted revenge. They threw him into a pit, sold him into slavery, and Joseph ended up in prison.

While Joseph was imprisoned, his interpretation of dreams resulted in him being brought before the king. His journey took him from the pit to the palace. Joseph interpreted the king's dreams and the King promoted him to second in command of the nation. He literally saved the nation from a national disaster. By the way, his brothers did bow before him. Joseph spared his brothers lives and the conclusion of the story was a happy ending. He was restored to fellowship with his family.

In the New Testament, after the virgin Mary gave birth to Christ, an angel appeared to Joseph in a dream warning him to flee immediately. Herod's plot to kill the promised Messiah failed. God used a dream to protect the Christ child... His only Son.

God has communicated through dreams in our family in every generation. Our son, Dana was excited about going on a picnic excursion to the Smokey Mountains with the other children from our church. The morning of the trip, when it was time to board the bus, he came to his dad and said, "If you don't want me to go, I won't go."

After they left, I noticed Herschel praying in his office. He had dreamed three nights in a row that Dana fell from a high place. He was troubled and decided to try to join them. We started driving. Just before arriving at their destination, a terrible storm came up and their bus had to pull off the road. The delay caused us to arrive at the same time they were getting back on the highway. We followed them into the canyon.

Dana was always an adventurous child. He ran constantly. There were no guardrails at the cliffs. Herschel didn't allow him out of his sight. It is imperative to understand the difference between a nightmare and being sensitive to a God-given message through a dream. He always believed the dreams saved our son's life.

Years later, Dana was praying early one morning and had a vision of his son Blake being hit by a car. Dana prayed for his safety. That afternoon, I took my grandchildren out to a nice restaurant for dinner. In the parking lot, Blake stepped right in front of a moving vehicle. An angel had to have been present. It was such a close call that it left all of us shaking.

We gave thanks to God all the way to the church. When Blake walked into his dad's office, he was upset and crying. Our other grandson, Michael exclaimed, "Your son was almost killed today!" Dana said, "I know. I prayed for him this morning. Thank God! He answered my prayer."

Almost every day, I drive through a beautiful, upscale residential neighborhood. Every home is fabulous. My favorite has fantastic landscaping with an ornate gazebo, and a wrought-iron fence encircling the courtyard. The delightful gardens and massive trees exhibit splashes of vivid color with contrasting shades of green in our spring and summer seasons.

Nestled under the shade of the trees is a miniature cottage for a little girl. At night, there is always a light shining in the window of the little playhouse. When I passed this house, I always admired its beauty and imagined the wonderful family who lived in such an incredible estate.

One night, I had a strange dream. I recognized the home. Inside, I saw a woman in deep despair. She was sobbing uncontrollably. I didn't see her face. She was kneeling on the floor with her head in her hands, facing a cement wall. It looked like a prison and felt like a dungeon. The next day, the dream kept replaying in my mind. I prayed for her every time I drove by the house. For three consecutive nights I saw the same scene in a dream. After the third night, I felt compelled to put some action to my concern.

It took all the courage I had to walk up to those front doors and ring the bell. A woman dressed in a white terry cloth robe came to the door. Her eyes were red from crying. I told her about the dream and asked if I could pray with her. She explained that she had just been released from the hospital and was in a desperate situation.

I told her that God must love her very much to speak to me in a dream. I assumed she was sick. She didn't invite me in or share any of the details. She just thanked me for coming. After prayer, I gave her my phone number and invited her to church. She never called. I didn't see her again, but I didn't forget her and continued to include her in my prayers. Walking in obedience to God is a team effort. One person plants the seed, another waters it through prayer and encouragement, and sometimes we get to witness the miracle.

Months later, my son and I were driving by that same house. There was an 'Open House For Sale' sign in the yard. I told Dana about the dream and we stopped and toured the home. When I looked outside through the windows in the family room, I was shocked. Instead of seeing a beautiful back yard, the view was a gray concrete block wall. There was only about a six foot wide walkway between the house and the wall. Apparently, the cement blocks were there to keep the hill behind the house from eroding. It was the exact scene that I saw in the dream.

The realtor said that there had been a divorce and the owners were forced to sell the property. The house had a sad, heavy atmosphere. As we were walking away, I literally felt the agonizing pain of the woman who had lived there. I prayed, "Dear God, only you know the depth of this woman's despair. You heard her desperate cries. Thank you for allowing me to have a small part in reminding her that you care."

I wonder how many times has someone prayed for you or me that we didn't even know? God's love is immeasurable. Whether it is a next door neighbor, someone on the other side of the globe, or your house, His love finds a way to reach each of us. He knows where we are.

The power of prayer
is the greatest power on earth.

"If My people
who are called by My name
will humble themselves,
and pray and seek my face,
and turn from their wicked ways,
then I will hear from Heaven,
and will forgive their sin
and heal their land."
-2 Chronicles 7:14

CHAPTER SEVEN
THE CHALLENGE

Last night, these words unexpectedly appeared in my mind like crawlers rolling across the bottom of a television screen. The subject was not on my original list, but I realized it was the title of my next chapter. I opened my iPad and the words began to flow. The whole world seems to be facing insurmountable challenges. Someone, somewhere, including myself, is needing to hear the words, "God knows where you are."

The America we live in today is not the same as the one in which I grew up. You don't have to watch CNN and FOX news very long to realize we have become the divided states of America. The conflicting, controversial media reports reveal the vast canyon of differences dividing the citizens of this nation. The chasm between the liberal and conservative agendas is becoming catastrophic.

We are facing the ultimate challenge because there seems to be no common ground and the reality is that, *"United* we stand and *divided* we fall." The foundation on which our country was founded is being threatened and in jeopardy. The question is not, "Is God on our side?" The question is, "Are we on God's side?"

The instability that is permeating the globe has saturated the atmosphere, and there is nowhere to go in which to escape the rising tension. Nations are afraid because of the uncertainty about what tomorrow may bring. Fear of things that could come to pass is invading the conversations in the marketplace. Globally and locally there is a feeling of unrest.

What an exciting time to be alive! Do you realize that God placed us in this generation on purpose? The greater the battle, the greater the victory. The greater the difficulty, the greater the miracle. I believe this generation will see the miraculous in an unprecedented fashion. I can hardly wait to see what God is going to do next. I believe that God is calling and preparing a new generation of bold believers who are rising up like an army to take the message of the Church of Jesus Christ to a new spiritual dimension.

We are entering a new realm where petty personal agendas will become insignificant. There is far too much at stake. Instead of being called *"The Young and The Restless,"* this generation will be known as *"The Young and The Relentless."* They are a modern, fearless "Joshua-generation" who know their God.

They are enlisting for active duty to face spiritual warfare in a world where anti-Christ and anti-God forces are advancing; where immorality is on the increase; where rebellion is running rampant. It is an age of violence like those of us who grew up in America have never seen.

But God! Don't ever rule out God! God has the power to rule and over-rule. He has the answer to every challenge that exists. Whether the battles we face in our daily lives at home, or abroad on the global scene, God has always been and He will always be present in every crisis. In the midst of your greatest challenge... when you are feeling totally alone, He is there.

I remember ironing a red silk robe I had been given for Christmas. Most fabrics are wash and wear, but this one had wrinkles on top of the wrinkles. I began to weep and felt impressed to pray for someone in China. I turned the iron off and knelt in front of my couch. The intensity of the prayer was exhausting. When I returned to the ironing board, I was surprised to see on the label, these words: "Made in China."

Only eternity would reveal the desperate situation for which I was praying... God knew! He said in Jeremiah 33:3, "Call to me, and I will answer you, and show you great and mighty things, which you do not know."

The next week I read a book about the persecuted church in China. It contained heartbreaking stories about Christians who are being imprisoned or are beaten because of their faith. They are forced to work as slaves making many of the products that are sold in our stores in America. I had no idea. I realized I was praying that day for the person who made my robe. I could not iron the robe without feeling the pain of the one who sewed every stitch.

God let me partner with someone in prayer whom I have never forgotten. I'm sure many people have prayed for you and me whom we have never met. Our greatest challenges prove the greatness of our God. He answers our prayers. The family of God is connected through His Holy Spirit who dwells within us. Together, we come through every trial with greater courage and the faith to face the next confrontation and assignment.

Recently, my daughter bought an item at a local store. When Deana opened the box, she noticed a note that had been handwritten in Chinese. She discarded it since she didn't know what it meant. Later, she read on Facebook about someone who had a similar experience. The person had the note translated into English and discovered that it was a desperate cry for help from a prisoner in China. The realization of what she may have held in her hand was shocking. Praying for others can also be life changing for us.

Deana remembered viewing a graphic television newscast reporting prisoners lined up in front of an execution squad singing, *"Amazing Grace."* If that doesn't touch your heart, nothing will. Years ago, I read a book titled, *"Let My Heart Be Broken... with the things that break the heart of God."* The book impacted my life. It placed the words, "Take time to pray," on the top of my daily list of goals.

Desperate needs call for desperate measures. It is time to fast a meal and spend time in prayer for those who do not understand. Our world is not going to change without a knowledge of God. Prayer is the most powerful force on earth. There is no distance in prayer. While kneeling in my living room, the answer to my prayer can travel to the darkest jungle in Africa... Wow!

One morning, Michael told his dad that he felt God wanted him to go to China. Dana said, "Sure son, someday." Michael said, "It will be soon Dad, not someday." Dana turned on his DVR to the Christian station. When he returned that evening, a major ministry was on the screen talking about their next trip to China. Dana called and inquired about the possibility of Michael going on the trip. He was informed that since he was only sixteen, he would have to accompany him. Within two days, Dana and Michael were preparing to go to China. It was a life-changing experience for both of them.

They returned with compassion for the precious Asian people. It was an unforgettable event. They would never be the same. Most Americans have never had to face the challenges and deprivation many people in other countries are experiencing. I believe a spiritual awakening is coming to shake us out of our comfort zone. It is past time for a narcissistic society to face the challenge to prepare for the inevitable turbulence that is on the horizon.

Together, we can face the adversity in "our world" both individually and corporately. We need each other. God knew my location that morning. While He was with me at my ironing board in Canton, Ohio, He knew the address of someone in China who needed my prayers. He allowed my daughter to hear a desperate cry for help through a note she had held in her hand. God is talking to us. Are we listening? God is always listening.

Recently, I was missing my mother and wishing I could ask her to pray with me. An amazing thing happened! I remembered, after her death when it was my turn to choose something that belonged to her, I asked for her ironing board. Having seven children, she had spent countless hours ironing. God reminded me of the many prayers she prayed for me in that exact same place...at her ironing board. My mother went to Heaven years ago and we are seeing many of those prayers still being answered. God keeps His promises.

This chapter was written to remind you that He is there. Someone may be praying for you today. My youngest grandson is a big six foot, two inches tall weight lifter. One day when he was working out in the gym, a man collapsed and it appeared that he was having a heart attack, Blake rushed over and asked to pray for him while they waited for the ambulance. Afterwards, someone came to him and said, "That was powerful." The power was not in his muscles that day. The power was in his prayer. The man said he admired his courage to step forward in front of all those body builders and proclaim his faith in God.

I don't know what challenges you are facing today but God knows. You are not alone. Don't give up. The answer is on the way. Keep your trust in God. Psalm 16:8 decrees, "I have set the Lord always before me; Because He is at my right hand I shall not be moved,"… or shaken. God knows where you are.

Don't let go of your dreams.
Glance at the problem.
Focus on the promise.

Jesus said,
.."With God all things are possible."
-Matthew 19:26

CHAPTER EIGHT
THE LION

My son was always impressed with the King of the Jungle. He has a lion collection. At our family reunion some of us took a trip to the Precious Moments Gallery in Carthage, Missouri. A huge ceramic lion caught my attention. It had these words inscribed on the side, "I will lie down and and sleep in peace." I kept going back admiring it but it was way out of my price range. When it was time to leave the store, I felt compelled to buy it anyway. I had no idea it was a message from God for a crisis we were about to face in our family.

That summer, our granddaughter, Allison, started having pain in her chest. Her pediatrician didn't think it was serious but ordered blood tests. The pain became more excruciating. She began losing weight rapidly. Her blood tests showed red flags, so they did extensive testing. She was diagnosed with lymphoma. Allison asked to stay when they met with the oncologist. He explained the spots on her lungs and behind her heart, and gave her three weeks to live. My son asked the doctor, "How sure are you?" The doctor replied..."Ninety-nine-point-nine percent." Dana said, "Then, I'll believe for the one percent." Allison asked, "Are you looking for cancer, because I'm looking for a miracle? I'm only nine years old. God isn't through with me yet."

They decided to perform an exploratory surgery. A surgeon in our church explained, "A diagnosis is a fact, but the Bible declares that nothing is impossible with God. His truth changes the facts!" Believe the report of the Lord, "Bless the Lord … Who heals all your diseases," Psalm 103, 2,3.

Hundreds of people were praying for Allison. At church on Sunday, she stood on the stage with her daddy and believed God for a miracle. She sang, *"Look what the Lord has done!"* When her aunt took her to buy new pajamas for the hospital. Allison said, "Take me to see the prom dresses. It will be awhile, but I will wear one!"

Her dad took her to Toys R Us and told her to pick anything she wanted. She chose a stuffed lion and named it, 'Courage.' One of the medical specialists gave her a big teddy bear. She named it 'Miracle.' A friend gave her a bear with a bumble bee on its nose and she named it 'Be Healed.' She had all three with her at the hospital. She could only take one into the surgical suite. She said, "I will leave Miracle and Be Healed, because I know God will take care of me." She held Courage, the Lion as she left to face the surgical procedures.

The night before the surgery, I remembered the Precious Moments lion I planned to give Dana for Christmas. The message on the inscription said, "I will lie down in peace, and sleep." I gave it to Dana as a gift from God. The next morning three people, from different parts of the country called and said, "Allison is going into the lions den, but she is coming out."

Jesus Christ, who is referred to in the Bible as *'The Lion of the tribe of Judah,'* went with her. Family and friends, including the father of the little girl Nan saved from drowning, waited and prayed through the whole ordeal. Hours later, when the surgery was completed, the doctor rushed out with a smile on his face. He said that every place there had been a tumor, there was only a scar. It was as if someone had performed laser surgery. There was no other explanation. It was a miracle! Her blood count returned to normal. She gained her weight back and had no more pain. Three weeks later, she returned to school.

Allison's dream came true. She and Hunter met in their early teens at a church conference. It was an emotional day when she was escorted to her high school prom with "the love of her life." Allison graduated from college with honors. There was not a dry eye in the audience when she shared this phenomenal miracle in her Valedictorian speech. Allison married the man of her dreams.

They both minister on our Cathedral of Life staff. They now have a beautiful daughter. Her birth was amazing. God chose Isabella Faith's birthday. Although she arrived several days past her due date, she was right on time. The woman in the birthing suite next to Allison was broken hearted. She had been told her baby girl would be stillborn because she no longer had a heartbeat. All day, while they were giving birth, our family prayed for both of them.

Hunter and Allison's daughter, Isabella, was born first. Hunter said, "Keep praying. We are believing that when the baby who has no heartbeat is born and laid on her mother's breast, a miracle will happen. The baby will breathe!" It was a shock and awe moment! It happened!!! The baby girl named Grace began to breathe, and she is perfect. I am now anxiously awaiting the arrival of my second great-granddaughter. Isabella is going to be a big sister. "Look what the Lord has done!"

Nothing is impossible with God. The next chapter will be Allison's journey through the eyes of a nine year old. God answers prayers, and "dreams still come true." ... Don't give up on your dreams. He knows where you are.

CHAPTER NINE
THE PROM-ISE DRESS
By: Allison Fowler

As I walked into the hospital, the chill of the air conditioner caused goose bumps to cover my body. I had lost fifteen pounds in a period of two weeks, and even the ninety-two degree weather of August couldn't warm me. My frail frame and lack of energy was evident to everyone around me, yet they continued to tell me that everything would be okay; or at least that's what their words said. Worry, fear, and the uncertainty of future events were written in their eyes in spite of their forced smiles.

I appreciated their attempt at a positive attitude, but it certainly didn't make the gut wrenching pain cease. Today was the day- the day that would either quench the dreams of my childhood, or the day that would propel me to reach even higher heights with what life I had left to live. We walked into the private room and, as I waited, I was so uptight I could feel my blood pumping through my veins. My heartbeat was as percussive and amplified as the sound of a war drum, and the look on my parents faces started to break what confidence I had left. When I heard the knock on the door, I clenched my jaw in an attempt to brace myself for the doctor's report.

The oncologist walked in carrying a large yellow envelope that I knew held the results of the previous tests. He took out the contents and displayed them for my parents and I to see. "I'm afraid I have some bad news." He added, with a look of concern, "You have lymphoma." The air was sucked out of the room, but for some reason which was unknown to me, I had a strength rise from within. He continued speaking, "As you can see, tumors have filled your lungs and heart."

The room was silent for a moment, but the faith in my heart continued to increase even though the news only got worse. He went on to tell us that I had three weeks to live. My parents didn't speak a word to each other, but tears streamed down their pale faces. I could tell they were trying to be strong for me, but I almost felt worse for them than I did for myself. The doctor scheduled an exploratory surgery and another biopsy for the next Thursday to see if they could prolong my life, and we left the hospital.

That night as I slept in my bed, I dreamed of the day when I would go shopping for a prom dress, and the day I would walk down the aisle to the man I love. Would I ever get to see that day? Little did I know, that as I slept, my family was standing around the bed, praying for a miracle. I grew up in church, and always believed there was a God, but never really pursued a personal relationship with Him wholeheartedly.

My parents had enough faith for both of us. Dad pastors a church and I had seen multiple people healed of deadly diseases, but now that it was a reality for me, it was a whole different story. The rest of the week, my parents spent a lot of time with me. I could tell that they were trying to make the best of the situation. They tried to complete my every wish. They wanted me to enjoy every day to the fullest.

The day arrived that I was to have my surgery and I was a little nervous. I had never been sick for more than two or three days before all of this. I wasn't used to having health issues. I certainly was not used to being pricked by needles or spending long hours in the hospital. I couldn't tell if it was just nerves or my memory, but somehow I had forgotten that I was even in pain from the lymphoma... Or maybe the pain had just subsided for a little while.

Regardless, it was time for me to lie down on the operating table and let the doctor do his job. I kissed my parents and they walked out of the room. The nurses asked me to put the mask over my mouth for anesthesia and count to ten... "One..two.....three......." The pauses between each number became longer and longer until I couldn't keep my heavy eyelids from shutting. My parents paced the waiting room for hours. Everyone was there. My parents, my brothers, my grandparents, and aunt anxiously pondered what was to come.

All of a sudden, the operating doors flew open! The surgeon was running toward my parents and barely stopped in time to keep from colliding with them. He was out of breath as a mysterious smile covered his face. He was saying, "It's not there! It's not there! It's a miracle! I've never seen anything like it." He continued to tell my parents that it looked like someone had removed every tumor with a laser. There were scars where each tumor used to be, proving they hadn't misdiagnosed me. I was totally and completely healed.

This experience changed me for the better. I will never be the same again. It taught me to live each day as if it were my last because life is a valuable gift that should not be taken for granted. Since then, out of a grateful heart, I have pursued my God-given destiny. God has proven Himself to be faithful. I was even blessed to be able to fulfill my childhood dreams of going to the prom with the same man to whom I am now married. I never want to miss an opportunity to leave a legacy, to show God's love and to inspire people around me.

We must remember to appreciate and enjoy our family and friends. Never pass down a chance to say, "I love you and I'm thankful for you." This trial had many obstacles to overcome, but more importantly, it taught me life lessons that have propelled me forward. It proved to me that "I can do all things through Christ who strengthens me," Philippians 4:13.

——I asked my granddaughter, Allison, to write the story in her own words, so we could envision what happened through her eyes. What a miracle!

Recently, I received a shocking phone call that one of my sisters was facing the same life threatening crisis. I flew to North Carolina to be with her for her second chemo treatment. The doctor said it was an aggressive cancer, but strangely, hadn't followed the usual pattern. As she disappeared behind the door an African American lady walked up to me and said, "God told me to tell you, Mary is going to be okay." That day, we received both the report of the facts and the report of the Lord. After eight treatments, the cancer was gone.

When God says something, it is so! And it is so, because God said it! Find a promise from God for whatever you need. *Glance* at the problem. *Focus* on "the promise." Repeat this after me: "I believe God's promises. It's going to be okay!" God's GPS knows where you are.

This is God's perfect will for your life:

"Beloved, I pray
that you may prosper in all things
and be in health,
just as your soul prospers."
-Third John 1:2

CHAPTER TEN
THE WISH

It was a normal busy morning. As I was taking care of business as usual, suddenly, it felt like the room was spinning. My blood pressure shot up to stroke level. I started experiencing pain in my chest and left arm. My doctor advised me to go straight to the hospital. I asked, "Can I go home first?" He said, "No, you could die."

In route to the hospital, Dana called asking what was happening. I said, "You're in Africa! You don't need to be worrying about me. Who told?" He said, "God did. I was praying and felt I needed to call home." He prayed for me and assured me that I would be all right.

The doctors ordered all the routine blood tests, an EKG, and a stress test. I felt calm until they asked me to sign papers releasing the hospital of liability in the event of a massive stroke or fatal reactions to the Heart Cath procedure. Since I am allergic to iodine, I waited to sign the papers until the next morning. Deana addressed my fears and asked God to give me peace.

My precious daughter stayed with me until I fell asleep. I wished Dana was there too, but that was impossible. I am so blessed to have two children with great faith. I had the assurance that God would either give me a miracle or the courage to face any negative test result. I dismissed fear.

Before leaving the room, Deana left the TV on the Christian station in the event I woke up during the night. At exactly 2:00 a.m. I woke up for no reason. I opened my eyes and was surprised to see Dana's face on the television screen. He hosted a show on TBN periodically. This program was several years old. I turned up the volume and he was telling the story about Daniel in the lions den.

In Daniel, chapter seven, the King made a decree that could not be reversed. When Daniel defied that law and refused to deny his faith in God, he was thrown into a den of raging lions. God sent an angel to the rescue, who literally closed the mouth of the lions. Can you imagine the surprise when the King found Daniel alive and well? He made another decree commanding the entire nation to serve the God of Daniel.

Dana said, "Your situation may feel like a lion's den, but Jesus Christ, the King of Kings and His angels are in the room. When He makes a decree, His words will come to pass. With God, all things are possible! You will live and not die! You are not going through this alone." By the time he got through preaching, I was ready for a lion's den. While my son was halfway around the world, God had arranged for him to be in my hospital room in Canton, Ohio, via electronics. He heard me make a wish... How incredible is that! God turns impossible situations into possibilities.

Since Dana wasn't even scheduled to be on that program, we called the TV station to inquire how it happened. The station manager discovered that because of technical difficulties with the currently scheduled broadcast, the program operator had to quickly find another show to put on the air. God orchestrated the entire event. He impressed my daughter to leave the TV on that station and even woke me up so I wouldn't miss the program.

That morning, when the young man taking me for the test checked my name tag, he asked, "Are you Pastor Dana's mother? Can I pray with you?" He prayed out loud all the way down the elevator, in front of everyone. When I arrived for the Heart Cath, I heard a voice on the loud speaker quoting the ninety-first Psalm. I knew God was there. The pain left and my test results were normal.

Whatever we have to face in life, God is faithful. Miracles are wrapped in many packages. Two of my sisters had to go through open heart bypass surgery. God used heart specialists to perform the answer to their problem. It is easy to believe that God, Who created everything that exists can do anything. But I have learned that the greatest faith trusts God, no matter what happens and however He chooses to answer my prayer.

The Bible declares in Ephesians 3:20 that "He is able to do exceedingly, abundantly above all that we ask or think"..*or wish*..."according to the power that works in us." God knows your thoughts. He knows where you are.

CHAPTER ELEVEN
THE CHRISTMAS PRESENT

It was Christmas Eve. I had decided to surprise my parents and spend Christmas with them in Kansas. Herschel and the children were traveling all night to spend Christmas with his family in Mississippi. Deana was crying because she didn't want to leave me. We decided to let them open their gifts before they left. Her gift was a baby doll that laughed out loud. The minute she heard the laughter, she exploded into giggling, but the tears were still rolling down her cheeks as they drove away. I had never been away from my children. As the car disappeared, I regretted my decision, but it was too late to change my mind.

I felt totally alone. I said, "God, it feels like even you are so far away that if I screamed as loud as I could scream, you couldn't hear me." The next morning when my friends arrived to take me to the airport, I was dreading the trip and wishing I had gone to Mississippi. At the same time I didn't want to disappoint my parents.

After boarding, I asked the flight attendant, "Is it too late to get off the plane?" She said. "No, but you can't get your luggage." I explained to her that I was just having mixed emotions. I actually couldn't imagine not being with my children for Christmas. Before take-off, she stopped to let me know they would be closing the door shortly. I smiled and said, "It's okay."

The lady next to me said, "God knows what is best. I'm sure your parents will be happy to see you." I closed my eyes and began to focus on Christmas in Kansas with the old fashioned pine tree and it's tinsel and bubble lights, the green and red crepe paper hanging from the ceiling in the front room, and the look of surprise on mom and dad's face when I walked into the house.

As the plane was taxiing down the runway, these absurd words went through my mind: "God, if it wasn't your will for me to go to Kansas, you could speak to the pilot to turn the plane around and take me back to the airport, and he could even get my luggage off." The plane stopped and I thought it was waiting for clearance before take off.

The craziest thing happened. I watched the plane divert from its course, turn, and head back to the gate. The cockpit door opened. The pilot spoke to the flight attendant. It didn't even occur to me what was happening. They walked straight back to where I was sitting. He smiled and asked if I was the young lady who wanted to get off the plane? In total shock, I answered, "Yes." He said, "Merry Christmas...and we are going to get your luggage for you."

Instantly, I knew God had read my thoughts. It is inconceivable that God went to all this trouble to let me know I don't have to say a word. He is closer than my skin. He knows every thought and will never leave me even for a moment. Even after all these years, I am overwhelmed. All I know is that it happened and the only explanation is one word..."God!"

My friends were eating breakfast in the airport cafe that overlooked the runway. They watched the plane return and saw me get off the plane. As they approached my gate, they were laughing in disbelief. I said, "I just got my first Christmas present. I'm going to Mississippi." The ticket agent booked me on the next flight out and rescheduled my flight to Kansas. He handed me the tickets and said, "Merry Christmas!"

I called my brother to explain the changes in my flight schedule. He works for American Airlines. He said, "This doesn't happen! Even if there had been an actual emergency, they would not have taken time to get your luggage off." Every time I tell this story I am amazed all over again!

"Delight yourself also in the Lord, And He shall give you the desires of your heart," Psalm 37:4. God knows your wish list. We don't have to wait for December 25th. We can celebrate the birth of His Son every day. Every morning that you wake up is a gift from God. "Merry Christmas!" He may even have a Christmas present waiting for you today. He knows where you are.

CHAPTER TWELVE
THE SPIDER

Once upon a time, a mother gave birth to a baby girl. She was so small, her grandmother put her wedding ring on her wrist for a bracelet. She used a man's handkerchief for a diaper and laid her in a shoebox. It was a high risk, traumatic pregnancy because of a poisonous black widow spider bite during the seventh month. The mother almost died. The baby quit growing after that episode.

When it was time for her to be born, the doctor came to the house. After her birth, he told the family, "I'm sorry the baby will die." They placed her on the oven door to keep her warm. Friends from the church gathered around the stove and prayed. God performed a miracle! The baby lived! They named her, "Gail," and that is the beginning of my story.

My grandmother lived with us. There were seven children in our family. She loved everyone, but me. She couldn't tolerate my presence in the room. Because of the tension, I was often excused from the table and my sister and I ate our meals in the family room. After school I stayed at the library until my parents came home from work. I went to my room when Grandma was upset. I spent many of my summers with relatives. I just assumed her animosity toward me was my fault.

As a child, God became my best friend. I talked to Him about everything. I never doubted His love. Someday, I would grow up, get married, and have children of my own. It wasn't until I was an adult that the impact of those years surfaced. I decided my parents must not have loved me. I couldn't imagine allowing my children to go through any abuse. Rejection and isolation produce emotional instability. This kind of inner conflict and struggle requires an inner healing. Absolutely, my parents loved me. What I was interpreting as rejection, in reality, was protection.

Health issues occurred that required me to have a hysterectomy. The medication prescribed to stop the hemorrhaging had the possible side-effect of suicidal thoughts. Unresolved issues from the past emerged and I became irrational. I wanted to go to heaven. I had thoughts of getting into my car in the garage and turning on the ignition. I wrote a letter to God explaining how I felt and asked for forgiveness. At 4:00 a.m. God woke up a friend and told her to call me, immediately. When she asked, "What is going on?"... it shocked me back into reality. I knew God had read the letter.

I went back to the office. A plaque on the wall said, "When you get to the end of your rope, tie a knot and hang on." Suddenly, my attention was drawn to a tiny spider crawling on the floor. I remembered that I could have died the day I was born, but God had other plans. "There is a time to be born and a time to die." God had not granted me either choice.

The next week, there was a story in the newspaper about an entire family dying from gas fumes that had gone from their garage throughout the whole house. That same scenario could have happened in our family. God sent a little spider and a phone call which possibly saved all of our lives. I spent the next week in the home of a minister in Atlanta, who was also a Christian psychologist. He led me through inner healing. It changed my life.

I didn't know until I was forty years old that my grandmother tried to convince my mother to have an abortion. Knowing the problem existed before I was born released me from feeling responsible for her issues. Recently, I asked God, "Why," and the answer flashed through my mind like a neon sign. Grandma thought the black widow spider was a sign of a curse. Her childhood had been infiltrated with fear and a distorted belief system involving witchcraft and superstition. Prior to her death, she placed her trust in Jesus Christ and received the peace only God can give.

At a Mothers Day luncheon, I asked each lady to bring something that was given to them by their grandmother. I had nothing to bring. That night, I dreamed that my grandmother was standing at the end of my bed. She was smiling. Her hands were outstretched and she was holding a ceramic powder dish. The next morning, I described it to my mother. In the dream it was a figurine of a man and woman. My memory of the image of the figurine that had always sat on her dressing table didn't include a man. The lid was the bodice of the woman and the powder was held in her skirt.

My mother mailed it to me. I was shocked when I opened the package. It looked exactly like the one in the dream! I have no explanation. I only know that the incident brought another dimension of healing. My grandmother will be waiting for me in Heaven, healed and whole.

I'm sure there is not one person reading this story, who hasn't experienced rejection on some level. Abandonment can present itself in many forms. It is designed to rob us of a healthy, self-image. Its assignment is to create emotional dysfunction and breed inferiority. I refuse to allow abandonment or rejection from any source to dictate my self-worth and threaten my purpose and destiny. My value was established by my Creator. My significance cannot be diminished by the opinion of any other person on the planet.

When I was a teenager, the day before I left for college my sister, Donna, gave me a gift. It was the ring she saw my grandmother place on my wrist the day I was born. She said, "Every time you look at this ring, I want you to remember that God took care of you then and He is taking care of you now. He will never shake His head and walk out of the room because nothing is too hard for Him. Do not accept or repeat negative words spoken over you. Your circumstances doesn't change who God is! Your situation doesn't change who you are and it doesn't change God's purpose for your life!"

The rest of my story hasn't been written yet and neither has yours. I am not a victim and neither are you. Rejection is a "set-up" for a "set-back." Surprise it with a "come-back." Whether it came from a coach, a teacher, parent, grandparent, or family member, a friend or stranger, or even your spouse; your response is what matters. You can turn it around. Reject rejection!

Rejection cannot prevent you from fulfilling God's eternal plan for your life because God's love and acceptance is unconditional. He promised to be there every moment you need Him. You are not alone. He is taking care of *you* even now and He always will. It isn't over, until God says, it's over. God's GPS can even send a message through a little spider. He knows where you are.

Jesus said,
"I am the way, the truth, and the life.
No one comes to the Father
except through Me."
-John 14:6

"And you shall know the truth,
and the truth shall make you free."
-John 8:32

CHAPTER THIRTEEN
THE JULY 4TH WEEKEND

There are moments in life that mark reoccurring anniversaries of traumatic experiences. For years, I suffered with panic attacks. I have heard several United States Presidents quote the famous words of our 32nd President, Franklyn D. Roosevelt: "We have nothing to fear, but fear itself." I had no idea that this July 4th weekend, the meaning of these words would change my life.

Typically, on the anniversary of the signing of the Declaration of Independence, I would be excited about celebrating freedom. Ironically, I was at the hospital, distraught at even the possibility of being admitted. I signed the registration papers, hoping to see a doctor for anxiety issues and be released. My husband requested a specific doctor who had been recommended by friends.

Since it was a holiday weekend, the doctor was unable to see me until Tuesday. A decision was made for me to be admitted for observation and he would prescribe a sedative. While waiting to be taken to my room, I felt a sense of fear grip me at the thought of even being there. An African American woman who was also sitting in the waiting room walked over to me and whispered, "God knows right where you are." Those words gave me the courage to defy fear and confront my issues. The peace of God settled over me and the feeling of panic disappeared.

I knew that emotional disorders could result in being placed in the locked psych ward. I visit people in the hospital from our church routinely. It's part of my job, but I had never experienced it from this side of the bed. I was given a hospital gown and my street clothes were removed from the room. The nurse asked why I was there. I told her I was hyperventilating with panic attacks.

I pretended to take the medicine. I was concerned about side effects. I didn't think the doctor could accurately evaluate me if I was medicated. The patient beside my room was screaming and trying to remove his door from the hinges. Instead of being terrified at being in a locked facility, I was wishing for a lock on my door.

In less than three weeks, I was scheduled to speak in Tulsa, Oklahoma, at a Women's Conference on the subject, "Overcoming Rejection." I decided I would use the time to prepare and focus on my message. A family acquaintance who worked in mental health came by the next morning. She said,

"I see the medicine is working." When I told her I didn't take the medicine, she said that she had to inform the hospital staff, and I could possibly be sent to the Massillon State Mental Hospital for not being cooperative.

I took charge of my life and picked up the call button. I told the nurse why and what I had done, and asked her to inform the doctor. I called a friend in Florida, and explained my situation. She immediately contacted a doctor in Atlanta. He arranged for my family physician to have me released into his care. On Tuesday morning, I was on a flight to Georgia.

Through counseling therapy the doctor helped me to understand the root source of the panic attacks. I will be forever grateful for his wise counseling. As a child, I had been locked in a dark, damp cellar. Subsequently, when I faced any chaotic, terrifying dilemma, I struggled to breathe until I could get out of the room. My mind was repeating the same reaction to the childhood trauma in the cellar. I learned that I have a split second to choose to respond rationally. This is the key: "For God has not given us a spirit of fear; but of power and of love and of a sound mind," 2 Timothy 1:7.

Focusing on that "truth" produced freedom. The crisis that could have sent me over the edge of despair only became my deliverance. God knew exactly where I was that July 4th. He was ordering my steps. I missed the fireworks, but God gave me a new freedom to celebrate and I never had panic attacks again. After psychological testing, I was released without medication. Jesus said, "If the Son makes you free, you shall be free indeed," John 8:36. The following week I was speaking at the "Take Charge of Your Life" Conference.

After all these years, I just today realized that fear was the only lock on the cellar door. I was sent down the stairs for canned goods. The light switch was turned off. It was pitch black. The dirt floor and dirt walls felt like a grave. I was so paralyzed by fear that I couldn't scream or move. Eventually, someone found me, but the fear of being locked into any situation that was out of my control, had literally terrorized me from the day it happened. I faced fear that day and replaced it with faith.

Jesus spoke these words in John 8:32: "You shall know the truth, and the truth shall make you free." What is keeping you incarcerated? What is the lock on your door? Is it fear? Is it an addiction? Is it an inability to forgive? Is it unbelief?... When you face what is holding you hostage, you will take the first step toward being free. You are only one decision away from freedom. Take charge of your life. You can celebrate Independence Day every day. You can walk out of your prison today. You can be free! God knows where you are.

CHAPTER FOURTEEN

THE SURPRISE

Planning surprises is one of my favorite pastimes. When my son was seven years old, he invited his classmates on the school bus to his "Surprise" Birthday Party. I love surprises, but this time I was the only one surprised when the doorbell started ringing. While my neighbor baked cupcakes, I drew a donkey and the children played the "Pin the Tail" game... Why not plan your own party? Surprise your guests. Let them make a wish and blow out the candles. Celebrate and eat cake!

God's surprises are distinctly unique. They don't always come wrapped in gift boxes, but there is a card attached. The Scripture promises written in His Word are your gift cards. Every promise has your name inscribed... I was scheduled to fly to Atlanta one morning. My sister, Donna, called to pray with me before the trip. She said, "I asked God to give you a surprise today." While waiting for take off, the flight attendant asked, "Are you Gail Gammill? You have a new seat assignment. You have been upgraded to a VIP status." I'm thinking, "Very Important Person?"

I was sure it was a mistake, but I followed her to First Class. Wow! Big leather seats! Filet mignon for lunch! The people in coach were eating little sandwiches. Now, you know how long ago this happened. I always wondered why people pay more to sit in the front of the plane. I was so excited. This must be my surprise!

So we arrive in Atlanta and I have to get on a shuttle to my hotel. I had to stop half way and wait for another shuttle to my destination. A business man, who actually looked like a VIP was pacing back and forth, looking at his watch. He was waiting for a limousine. Finally, he went to a pay phone and called a friend. Before the limo arrived, his friend showed up and he left.

In a few minutes, this long, stretch, black limo arrives and the driver came inside. I said, "I think your client just left." He asked, "Where are you going?" When I told him the name of my hotel, he said he was going right by there. He asked if I would like to ride in his limo. Are you kidding me? I had no idea how important people live. He said, "Enjoy your ride. Help yourself to anything you want to drink." I was given royal treatment. I arrived in style and two men escorted me into the hotel. The clerk looked at my reservation and said that I had been upgraded to VIP status and I was given a magnificent suite on the top level... Only one elevator went to that floor.

Another surprise! I cannot describe what I was feeling. This is unbelievable! Anything I wanted to eat in the room was provided at no extra charge. I was given meal vouchers for the restaurant. Every meal was complimentary. I could eat whatever and whenever I wanted. When I called home and shared the unexpected details of my trip, everyone was shocked. No one knew how it happened. It was an unexplainable, inconceivable enigma. The mystery had only one answer—God! My sister asked Him to give me a surprise and He answered her prayer.

Prior to the trip, I had just been released from a horrendous hospital ordeal. I learned, "I can do all things through Christ who strengthens me." I passed a test. It was time for a celebration! God not only accompanied me on the trip, He planned a Surprise Party. The only ones on the guest list were my Heavenly Father, His Son, Jesus Christ, and His Holy Spirit. God's GPS was ordering and directing each event. He wanted me to know I am important to Him.

I wish you could know how much God wants to show you that He loves you. When extraordinary surprises arrive without an explanation, give God the credit. He expresses His love in inexplicable, creative ways letting you know He is there. He knows where you are.

The manner in which you view yourself
will determine
your success or failure.

When you see yourself through God's eyes,
you will see a winner!!!

CHAPTER FIFTEEN
THE RED DRESS

The story of *The Red Dress* was one of those "to be continued" lessons that kept resurfacing through the years with "the rest of the story." Each event played a significant role in my spiritual growth and development.

We had been sent to Salt Lake City to establish a church. The contrast of the spacious as-far-as-you-can-see wheat fields of my home state in Kansas to this beautiful metropolis surrounded by an array of majestic mountains out in the distance, was overwhelming. What an incredible display of the handiwork of God! What a wonderful place to build a church! My childhood dream came true. I began my role as the pastor's wife.

Some unexpected money arrived in the mail on Valentine's Day. Herschel took me shopping for a red dress. I had never owned a red dress. It was fun twirling around and modeling it for him. I thanked him for wanting to spend it on me, but I was sure we would need the cash for something more important. That night we were invited to dinner at the home of one of our parishioners. The lady of the house had grown up in a very strict environment. During the meal, she expressed a personal conviction that it was inappropriate and improper for a lady to wear red. I was thankful I didn't buy that dress. It would have offended her.

The next week I received a package in the mail. The card said, "I felt impressed to buy this for you." I said, "Now, what am I supposed to do? I can't wear this." Herschel said, "Obviously, God wanted you to have a red dress. Would you rather offend Him?" He told me that I could never please everyone. The only one I need to please is God. On Saturday night, I received a phone call. The same lady from church had been shopping. She informed me that she had changed her mind. She bought a new dress. Guess what! On Sunday, we were both wearing red.

When you don't learn the first time, sometimes you have to go around that same mountain again. Twenty years later, I'm still a busy pastor's wife trying to cross all the "t's" and dot all the "i's." Trying to be perfect is emotionally and physically draining. It is impossible! Stress can cause serious health issues. I was admitted to the City of Faith Hospital in Tulsa, Oklahoma for tests to discover why I was always exhausted. I had an amazing counselor who literally, radically changed my life with his words of wisdom from God's Word. "The counsel of the Lord stands forever," Psalm 40:11.

A woman I had never met came from ORU to pray with me. She addressed some personal painful issues. I knew that God sent her. She said God was healing all of my hurts and sending me to release healing to the broken hearted. She spoke as God's messenger and proclaimed that someday it would come to pass: "I would stand on a large stage in a red dress and declare the powerful Word of God to hundreds of women."

I knew the red dress symbolized my freedom to be me; freedom from intimidation and the unrealistic expectations of others; freedom from the fear of rejection. I never forgot those words. Years passed and one day, I thought I was ready. I bought a red dress. A few weeks later I was given an invitation to speak at a National Women's Conference.

Just before I left for my trip a seamstress in our church surprised me with another beautiful dress. She didn't have a pattern. God showed her the dress in a dream. It was like something Cinderella would wear. It was red satin with sequins. It fit perfectly. She had never heard my red dress story. I wore a red dress each day of the Conference.

It was amazing. Both dresses are still in my closet to remind me that God didn't forget His promise. His timing is always perfect. God will never forget "you." He promised! He knows where you are.

There is no greater love!

"For God so loved the world
that He gave His only begotten Son,
that whoever believes in Him
should not perish
but have everlasting life."
-John 3:16

CHAPTER SIXTEEN
THE MESSAGE

One of my favorite Hallmark slogans is, "Family is everything, and everything else is just everything else." I was privileged to grow up with four sisters and two brothers. Donna was the oldest sibling and she mothered all of us. I'm sure I wouldn't be the person I am today if God hadn't given me a sister like Donna. I thank God for every prayer she prayed for me and the luxury of being loved and taught by her. It was a privilege being her little sister. She was an impeccable role model.

We stayed in close contact through the years. We talked long distance almost every week. One day, she called and said, "I asked God to send you a message in an unusual way that He loves you today." It was my Wedding Anniversary and my family was coming for dinner. That afternoon, I realized I needed some things from the store. I was rushing to pick up groceries and remembered the phone call. I reminded God that I was still waiting for Him to tell me in a special way that He loves me. God always answered Donna's prayers. I wondered, "Did I miss it?"

Suddenly, the music on the store PA sound system stopped. The program was interrupted with Stevie Wonder's voice singing, *"I just called to say, I love you. I just called to say how much I care. I just called to say, I love you and I mean it from the bottom of my heart..."* And then as abruptly as it started, it stopped and continued the same song that was originally playing. I laughed out loud. Really? Stevie Wonder's voice interrupted the air waves like he was singing in concert and I was the only one in the audience! I thought, "I can never tell anyone this happened, ...they won't believe it." Doesn't God have a sense of humor?

While I was on my way home, I remembered my husband quoting the nine Beatitudes in a sermon. Matthew 5:8 records these words from Christ's famous Sermon on the Mount, "Blessed are the pure in heart, For they shall see God." Herschel explained that from the original Greek, it actually translates, for they shall see God, *"in everything."*

My daughter, Deana, arrived with a special gift. While I was at the grocery store, God was with her on a shopping trip in a nearby city. She was leaving a store and noticed a cup in the window. While walking to her car she felt compelled to go back, purchase the cup, and give it to me before dinner. The inscription said, "Blessed are the pure in heart for they shall see God." It was amazing. These kind of moments don't just happen.

My grandson, Michael, asked, "How big is God?" Really? How do you answer that question? He is everywhere at one time. He is the same yesterday, today, and forever. He is beyond amazing! He is more than wonderful... He is indescribable! How awesome that beyond all of His greatness, He loves us. Every time I use that cup, I am reminded that God loves me. The love of God is more than my mind can comprehend.

When our son, Dana, was studying theology in college, he asked his grandpa some questions about eschatology. He was always intrigued with prophecy and the Book of Revelation. Grandpa Gammill replied, "Son, I don't understand much about those things. All I know is that... *Jesus loves me, this I know, for the Bible tells me so.* That's all I need to know."

God's plan of the ages was set in motion before the beginning of time. He created the heavens and the earth with us in mind. Donna went to heaven this past year. My first thought when I woke up that morning was that I can't call Donna anymore. I looked at her cell phone number and felt a roller coaster of emotions. I didn't cry because she went to heaven. I cried because she wouldn't be at the family reunion. I can't call her today, but Heaven is real and I will see her again. The memories she leaves behind will continue to impact me until we are together again for all eternity.

If you are reading this and you are not sure you would go to heaven, you are a only a prayer away. John 3:17 tells us that God didn't send His Son into the world to condemn you. He sent His Son to save you. God sent you a personal text message in Acts 16:31: "Believe on the Lord Jesus Christ, and you will be saved, you and your household." It's just that simple.

God loves you more than you can imagine. He longs for a relationship with you. You can reach Him twenty-four hours a day. In fact, right now, right where you are sitting, you can invite Jesus Christ into your life through a sincere prayer.

"Dear God, I come to you in the name of Jesus. I believe. I thank You for sending Your Son. I accept Jesus Christ as my Lord and Savior for now and for eternity. I am so sorry for my sins. I receive Your unconditional love and forgiveness. Thank You for Your peace"... Simply talk to Him from your heart.

Welcome to God's forever family! God loves you. ... He knows where you are.

CHAPTER SEVENTEEN
THE CROSS AND THE SWITCHBLADE

The Cross and the Switchblade is the title of a book written by, David Wilkerson. It begins with David seeing a report of seven boys on trial for brutally murdering a fifteen year old polio victim. While the trial was in progress, he felt compelled to go to New York City and minister to them. Dave ends up being thrown out of the courtroom. His picture holding his Bible appeared in the news headlines. The trip opened his eyes to the existing gang wars and drug related violence.

Eventually, he left his country church, moved to the Big City, and founded a new ministry called, Teen Challenge. He miraculously acquired an old mansion with three floors at 416 Clinton Avenue in Brooklyn. He came to my Bible College seeking young people to live at the Teen Challenge Center and help reach out to these troubled teenagers. At first, it didn't even occur to me to be interviewed. In comparison to living in Kansas, New York City was like traveling to a foreign country on another planet in outer space.

In the meantime, I went on tour to New York City with the Revival Time Choir. I remember my first glimpse of the city. The vast Atlantic Ocean with its great ships, the Statue of Liberty posing as if I were taking its picture, and the millions of lights in the gigantic skyscrapers were breathtaking. I stayed with a girl whose father served on the NYPD. I stayed up all night listening to shocking stories and reading heartbreaking articles.

As we drove down the back streets of Brooklyn, a rock beat blared from dimly lit taverns. The streets were crowded and filled with more people than I had ever seen in one place. Drunks were laying in doorways and staggering around garbage cans in alleys. Groups of rough looking guys gathered in store fronts. There were girls standing on busy street corners dressed in bright, skintight clothing, puffing on cigarettes. They had an empty, hollow look on their faces. It broke my heart.

I knew I had to return. I was given permission to come at my own expense. Only God knew what I needed. He spoke to a family I had just met on tour to send me a check for seventy dollars. It paid for my plane ticket. I was on my way. This part of my life story would impact me for the rest of my life. I grew up in a very protected environment and had never even heard a curse word. We were required to go through intense training to prepare us for the shock of life on the streets.

Violence was a key word to remember in order to stay situationally aware. I witnessed gang wars and street murders. I saw the devastation of drug addiction, alcoholism, and sexual promiscuity. We spent our mornings in prayer. In the afternoon we were on the streets witnessing to young people in Brooklyn, Harlem, and the Bronx. It was our job to tell them that God loves them. It wasn't unusual for someone to say, "You're standing in my front yard. Go to hell." I couldn't imagine living on the streets in such dangerous surroundings.

Once, a man leaped from the shadows between two towering buildings and lunged to grab me. I stretched out my hand as if I was directing traffic at a stop sign. When I shouted, "Jesus," my voice echoed like it was being amplified in a loud speaker. For a moment, it was as if the man had become paralyzed in that position. There was a look of horror on his face. God must have allowed him to see my guardian angel. The last time I saw him, he was still running in the opposite direction.

We went to the same projects every week. It was fascinating seeing the Holy Spirit in action. I saw tough guys kneel on the street, drop their switch blades, and become radically transformed by the powerful message of the cross. I saw drug addicts delivered from mainlining heroin into their veins, and young girls turning away from addiction and lifestyles of prostitution.

We had a chapel on wheels. All day invitations to an evening street meeting were announced on loud speakers. The big bus with its massive flood lights would arrive and the entire side opened up, creating a platform. Hundreds of people would gather for our outdoor rallies. I always sang just before the message. They called Dave Wilkerson, "The Gang Preacher."

He spoke with compassion and gave an invitation to accept Jesus Christ. During the first month, five hundred teenagers accepted Christ. They dropped their drug habits. They left the gangs. Churches opened their doors to help mentor and develop relationships with many of them. We were able to bring some of them to the Teen Challenge Center and get them into a safe environment.

Miracles were ordinary daily events. When there were no groceries in the house, Dave told us to give thanks even though there was no food on the table. While we were praying, the doorbell rang. An elderly lady was standing at the door holding her piggy bank. It had the exact amount of money needed to buy our meals that day.

One morning, an eviction was inevitable if a past due note in the amount of $15,000 wasn't paid on the Teen Challenge Center "that day." We were in the chapel praying for another miracle when the doorbell rang. It was a Special Delivery. Inside the envelope was a certified check for $15,000. The check was tear stained as each of us held in our hand God's answer to our prayer. Every financial need was met with a miracle.

God shows up in the drama of our life and His unconditional love reaches out to the characters in each scene. Although David Wilkerson never got to meet those seven boys on trial that day, God used the experience to send him to thousands of others who were hurting. Our Heavenly Father is watching over us and meets every person at the point of their need.

Milta was a Deb and Doll war counselor in the Coney Island Bishop gang. She came forward and received Christ in the very first street meeting she attended. Immediately, she was receiving threats. As a precaution, David Wilkerson moved her into the Teen Challenge Center.

It was announced on loud speakers that a former Bishop would be giving her testimony in the Fort Green Projects. This was the rival Mau Mau and Chaplain territory. They sent a warning that they would be there to get her. The Chaplains stood with their switch blades. She was fearless. Milta walked out on the platform of the bus and boldly proclaimed that she was willing to die for Jesus. She shared a powerful testimony of how God had changed her life and walked away unharmed.

Francisco was known as the Phantom. He had seen and taken part in more gang wars than any other sixteen year old in Brooklyn. Frankie was a member of the Mau Mau gang. The night that he committed his life to Christ, he had a vision of two great hands preventing a speeding truck from hitting him. On the other side of the street, he saw the same two hands holding an open Bible.

When Frankie walked by the street meeting, he knew God was calling him before it was too late. His life was forever changed. He left the gang. Later the Mau Mau's were involved in a murder trial. If Frankie had continued living that gang lifestyle, he could have possibly been prosecuted with his friends.

It was the end of the summer. One by one young people shared where they would be "without the grace of God." Mike was on his way to a gig when he passed the street meeting. Dave Wilkerson said, "Son, God wants you." He gave his life to Christ that night. His friends went on to the party. One friend was killed and the other was knifed. He said, "It could have been me.

I realized that without Christ we would all be lost but with Him, thank God, we are saved! Our trust is in the living God. His Son, Jesus is the Savior of every person who believes. It would take an entire book to share all of the incredible miracles.

It was time to say goodbye. I thought about the skyline of this great city with all of its culture, material wealth, and crowded millions of people. I thought about how Jesus must have felt when He wept over Jerusalem. I remembered the words in Psalm 8:4, "What is man that You are mindful of him?" To try to fathom His greatness in our simple minds is overwhelming. The greatest miracle of all was the miraculous transformation in the lives of those hundreds of teenagers.

I thought about one night when I was waiting to sing at a street service in the Red Hook projects. A gang member grabbed me and was planning to interrupt the service by injecting me with a needle of heroin. Another addict, who was a member of the gang saved my life. Not only was I saved, but the drug addict committed his life to Jesus Christ.

It was astonishing seeing damaged, abused girls changed into pure, sweet Christians; drug addicts delivered and transformed into cleansed vessels with the desire to change their world; and tough, rebellious gangsters become meek personalities preparing to go to Bible School and preach the Gospel of Jesus Christ. Today, there are many Teen Challenge Centers throughout the world.

It's hard to believe that fifty five years have passed since I was witnessing to teenagers on the streets of New York City. Recently, while I was watching a national Christian television station, tears rolled down my cheeks as Sonny Arguinzoni was giving his testimony. I was there. I saw God change his life all those years ago. I still have vivid memories of the miraculous life-changing intervention of God in the lives of Nicky, and Sonny, Mary, Rosa, Lucky, Jose', Ralph… and the names go on and on of those who became "former" gang members, alcoholics, and drug addicts transformed by the powerful message of Jesus Christ and the Cross.

How many others are still waiting for someone to show them that Jesus is the answer? *"What can wash away my sins? Nothing but the blood of Jesus!"* If I had grown up in that environment my name could have appeared on that list. I was only four years old when I became a Christian. I never had to experience that kind of agonizing pain, but the deliverance is still the same. The moment we ask for forgiveness, a transformation happens; Jesus called it being "Born again."

The United States is now on a National High Alert because of a heroin and opiate epidemic. Ohio is one of the leading states with drug related deaths. Recently statistics reported that one hundred forty four Americans die every day from an overdose of drugs. That alarming number is continually rising. Drug abuse is affecting people of every age and from every walk of life. Medical science has no cure. Jesus Christ is the only answer.

There are pictures posted on Facebook by brokenhearted parents of children who died because of drug abuse. They are pleading with young people to not be deceived. It became a shocking reality at one of our street services when I witnessed a drug addict stab the chest of another teenager with his switchblade. We saw him fall to the ground and before the ambulance could arrive, we watched him curse away his last breath. We spent the night in the chapel weeping in prayer and intercession.

Marijuana is the leading drug that becomes the first step toward addiction. Heroin today is laced with other components. The person is hooked and often dies after the first use. Alcoholism is at an all time high. It kills brain cells and altars your ability to think and act rationally. Chemical dependence is not an answer. It can lead you down a path of no return. I witnessed first hand the destructive devastation it brings.

Drugs and alcohol will poison and destroy your mind. Their assignment is designed to rob you of your future. "Wine is a mocker, strong drink is raging, and whosoever is deceived thereby is not wise," Proverbs 20:1 KJV. The Bible warns us in Galatians, 6:7, "Do not be deceived, God is not mocked; For whatever a man sows, that he will also reap." Wisdom can see the reaping before the sowing. Don't sacrifice your tomorrows because of bad choices today. Choose wisdom.

If you or someone you know is facing an addiction crisis, get help before it is too late. If you ask God for wisdom, you will receive wisdom. God said in Deuteronomy, 30:19, "...I have set before you life and death, blessing and cursing; therefore choose life, that both you and your descendants may live." Heed the warning! Defy the consequences by changing your course. It's your choice.

The power of choice is a gift from God. When you choose life, God sends deliverance! It is incredible! God can take the most devastating experience in life and turn it into the platform on which you stand to declare your greatest victory. I watched it happen on the streets of New York City and it can happen for you on *"your"* street, in *"your"* home town...He knows where you are.

CHAPTER EIGHTEEN
THE DIVINE LOVE CONNECTION

Looking for a relationship?... One of my favorite questions is asking couples how they met. Have you wondered how people living on the opposite sides of the country get connected and fall in love at first sight? It is fascinating to look back and see the parade of circumstances or events that happen bringing two people into the exact same place at the same time. Coincidence? Some people would think I am too Pollyanna or a hopeless romantic. I believe when you ask for God's perfect will in your life, He will arrange a rendezvous with a perfect match. I think it is unimaginable that the Creator of the universe who created everything that exists with such precision and detail, would not have strategic plans for those He created.

My dad always said mom was the most beautiful woman he had ever seen. They were introduced by a mutual friend. We didn't know until we were grown up that mother was carrying an unborn child. She had been assaulted by a distant relative. Dad asked her to marry him the first time they met. She wasn't as impressed. He was dressed in farm clothes. She said, "I would never marry a man who wears overalls." Three weeks later, he showed up at her door in a new black suit and repeated the question. She said, "I don't love you." He said, "I have enough love for both of us." They were married for sixty three years. The baby was stillborn, but God gave them seven more children and a multitude of memories to cherish and hold dear for a lifetime.

My husband's parents met for the first time when they were sixteen years old. His dad loved telling the story. Walking down a country road, he saw a beautiful girl with long dark hair. He stopped, introduced himself and asked her if she would like to marry a preacher. He had already preached his first sermon. She said, "I don't know, but I'll ask my parents." They prayed with her and said they would give her an answer in the morning. The answer was "Yes." They repeated their vows beside a little creek. They raised four sons and were married for sixty four years. Thousands of people were connected to the love of God through their radio and pastoral ministry.

Herschel and I grew up a thousand miles apart. He attended Lee College in Cleveland, Tennessee, and I was a student at Central Bible College in Springfield, Missouri. During my summer break while I was ministering in New York City with

Teen Challenge, I met four students on the team from Lee College. When it was time to return to school, I decided to transfer to Lee to be a part of their Pioneers for Christ witnessing program.

My parents couldn't afford to pay for any of my tuition. David Wilkerson gave me two hundred and fifty dollars to cover my down payment. I remember being asked, "Who is responsible for the balance of your bill?" I said, "I am. The money will be here when it is due." I had seen so many financial miracles in New York City that I thought God could drop it out of the sky. He did! The day the bill was due, I was informed that someone had anonymously paid the entire amount of my first college semester.

When the second semester arrived, I had no down payment. The week before the deadline, I received a plane ticket to Owensboro, Kentucky with an invitation to spend the weekend with people I had only met once on a choir tour. These people were not entrepreneurs. They lived very modestly and gave sacrificially. Beyond their necessities, the rest of their salaries were given to support people in need around the world. They introduced me to the owner of the company where they worked. He gave me a check that paid the rest of my school expenses that year. I was overwhelmed! After all these years, I am still amazed! Faith touches the heart of God. Only believe!!!

That step of faith was a "Divine love connection." I met the man I would walk with down the aisle. During second semester, Herschel proposed and I said, "Yes." The first time he heard me sing, he told his friends, "I'm going to marry that girl." He went with me to New York City and joined the Teen Challenge team. As a little girl, it was my heart's desire to marry a minister. That summer, on August tenth, we had a wedding to attend and we began our ministry together. This year will be our 55th Wedding Anniversary.

There are no perfect relationships because people are imperfect. The good news is that God, who is perfect, can resolve conflicts and differences. God gives us the freedom of choice. Unfortunately, a successful marriage depends on the choices of *two* people. Someone may be asking, "What happens when your Plan-A doesn't work out?" When the circumstance is beyond your control, trust God with the outcome. God can heal broken hearts. It's not the end of your story. The greatest love of all is the unfailing *love of God*. He always has a plan.

I witnessed two of my neighbors go through a difficult season. Fred was suffering from a brain tumor and his wife, Diane, was fighting cancer at the same time. Their positive attitude and courage was amazing. I stopped by to encourage them, but realized, I left with more strength than I brought. I wondered, "How can anyone endure a situation this painful?" The answer was simple: Faith in God and their love for each other. The Bible says in Deuteronomy 33:25,27, "...As your days so shall your strength be; The eternal God is your refuge. And underneath are the everlasting arms." His strength will arrive the moment it is needed. God keeps His promises.

Fred shared an incredible story. His daughter who lives in Arizona was en-route to Canton, Ohio to help care for them during this crisis. It wasn't an accident that her seat assignment on the plane would place her next to the man she would marry. They exchanged phone numbers on the plane and stayed in touch. God planned for them to meet and they fell in love. Now that is what I call an arranged marriage! God granted Fred's desire. He attended the wedding ceremony before he entered the dawn of eternity with the peace of knowing his daughter was happily married.

Diane fully recovered. Recently, she told me that her daughter's husband also developed a brain tumor, several years later. As he experienced the same painful, traumatic illness, his wife was by his side. The surgery was successful." And the Lord God said in Genesis 2:18, "It is not good that man should be alone." God understands the need for relationship. Proverbs 18:22 says, "He who finds a wife finds a good thing, And obtains favor from the Lord." It's called "Divine providence."

My grandson, Michael, grew up in the same local church with the girl he married. He is five years older so they didn't notice each other growing up. When Jacee was fifteen years old she told her mother, "Someday I'm going to marry Michael Gammill." Michael expected to meet the girl of his dreams while he was attending college. It didn't happen, but Jacee grew up! After his graduation they became great friends and fell in love.

Michael had traveled in almost every continent. Jacee had hardly been out of Ohio. One summer, Michael took a group of people to teach students in the Livingston, Zambia schools. Jacee was a part of the team. She had no idea he brought an engagement ring. He proposed near the Victoria Falls in Zimbabwe. Halfway around the world, sitting under a Monkey tree at a table sprinkled with rose petals, and zebras in the background of their pictures... Jacee said, "Yes."

God is the original wedding planner. I believe if you ask for God's guidance, He will bring that special someone into your life to compliment and bring out the best in both of you. I don't believe in coincidence. I believe in God. He is so awesome. I will never cease to be amazed at the way God orchestrates every little detail in our lives. His perfect timing has been bringing Divine Love Connections since time began. Ask for guidance. God knows where "you" are.

CHAPTER NINETEEN
THE UNLIMITED PROVISION

When my husband and I were first married, we decided to take a year off from Bible College. We were asked by our church organization to accept an assignment to start a church in Salt Lake City, Utah. Herschel was nineteen years old and we had been married thirty days when we arrived. We rented a storefront building to provide a worship center. Now, all we needed was a congregation.

The large front room surrounded with windows provided an auditorium. We began with forty chairs, a piano, and a pulpit. The small room in the back with cement block walls and no windows became our home. It had running water in a small bathroom. A curtain covered doorway separated the area from the front of the building. We had no furniture. We were sleeping on a mattress on the floor. I was so scared of spiders that I covered the holes in the floor with pots and pans. The first month's rent was paid for in advance, but all of the remaining expenses were a step of faith.

I was so excited! I said, "I think God is preparing us for the mission field." Herschel replied, "I think we're there!" Every day we knocked on doors and invited people to come to our church. We were in an area that was ninety percent Mormon. Our first family began coming to our church because there was no Catholic Church to attend. We started with five members. Our Sunday services grew to sixty five in attendance. We learned to trust God in the "classroom of life" that year.

Eighteen years later, we returned to Salt Lake City and were privileged to reunite with these precious families. We reminisced many miracles of God's supernatural provision for every need, including the meals on our table. Once, for three weeks we only had one small serving bowl of pinto beans. At the end of every meal, no matter how much we ate, the bowl still had the same amount of beans. One Sunday, after the morning service we shared our meal with a family of five. The miracle of the beans that kept multiplying before our eyes was an unforgettable phenomenon.

The day the beans disappeared, sitting at our back door was three big boxes of groceries. Repeatedly, there was very large amounts of cash mysteriously placed in a sea shell on our shelf. Money came in the mail from people we had never met. Bills we owed would arrive that were either reduced or marked paid. We were in awe. God is faithful!

Herschel worked the night shift in a factory. The previous week, someone had shot holes into the windows of our building. Through the curtain in my doorway, I could see the streetlight outside the front of the building. I was terrified when I saw a man trying to break into the front door. I kept my lights out and prayed. My neighbor turned on his porch lights. He called and told me to run out my back door. Suddenly, the surprise of the piercing sound of a siren caused the intruder to take off running in the opposite direction. The year we spent in Salt Lake City increased our faith in God and prepared us for all the years that followed.

Years later, my husband was assigned to fulfill a four year appointment as a National Evangelist. It meant that he would be traveling most of the time. We stayed at the Holiday Inn, because our house wouldn't be available for a month. When Herschel left for his first revival, I didn't even know how to drive a car. I was upset and crying because I didn't know how I was going to get Dana, our six year old son to school.

Dana said, "God knows!" We began praying and the phone rang. It was the owner of the home we were waiting to rent. Her mother had to leave because of an emergency. She asked if we could move in immediately and help her pack. Guess what? The school bus stopped at her front door! Three weeks later, I had my driver's license.

The new normal was overwhelming. Deana was only three. Every time Herschel left on a trip, they both cried. At the airport when she watched the plane disappear, I literally had to carry her to the car. She turned all of her toys upside down in her room and said, "I don't have a daddy anymore." I experienced the daily responsibility of raising the children by myself.

One morning, I knelt and asked God for wisdom. I was still crying as I walked into the kitchen to wash the dishes. All of a sudden, I heard myself singing. *"I have everything I need to make me happy. I have Jesus to show me the way. He loves me and gave me life eternal and now I have everything."* I threw the dish towel over my shoulder and praised God. Deana began marching like she was in the parade, laughing and singing with me. God provided us with an unlimited supply of wisdom, peace, and joy every time I asked.

Another day, both of the kids were crying. Dana was upset that his dad would miss a Father-Son event at school. Our doorbell rang announcing an elderly gentleman who was a personal friend with the owners of the house. He had left his fishing pole in the garage. The man told us he would be back." He returned with his wife and they set the children on their laps. He said they would be their grandparents while their daddy was away. They treated them like their own grandchildren.

They created weekly events to spend time with them. When Dana was in the seventh grade he had to write a paper about someone, other than a family member, who had influenced his life. Dana wrote about his "Grandpa Darter." God provided everything we needed... Even grandparents!

After losing his baby teeth, Dana was so excited when his permanent teeth finally arrived. Then a bicycle accident broke one front tooth, and both front teeth were barely attached. The nerves were dead and they turned black. The dentist said he couldn't save them. I said, "God will heal them!" Three weeks later, the teeth were intact and white. He said, "This is not possible. It's a miracle!!!"

While Herschel was traveling, I thought it was my job to protect my family. As soon as the children were asleep, I would sit in a rocking chair where I could see all three of the outside doors. After three weeks, I realized it was ridiculous. I thanked God for assigning an angel at each door and went to bed. There would be no intruders. He took care of me in Salt Lake City and He would take care of us in Cleveland, Tennessee.

The Bible promises in Philippians 4:19, "My God shall supply *all* your need according to His riches in glory by Christ Jesus." God's supply is *limitless* and His GPS can even deliver it to your front door. He knows where you are!

Today I will access God's promises.

"For I know the thoughts and plans that I have toward you, says the Lord; thoughts and plans for welfare and peace and not for evil, to give you hope in your final outcome."
-Jeremiah 29:11 Amplified

CHAPTER TWENTY
THE MIRACLE ON 38TH STREET

God prepared Herschel in advance for each new assignment. For years, his mission was to pioneer and build churches. We started our first church in Salt Lake City, Utah with five members and we were two of the five. The sanctuary in the church he built in Toms River, New Jersey could seat 160 people. It would almost fit into the prayer chapel of the church he built in Canton, Ohio.

In Birmingham, Alabama, the congregation grew so rapidly, it became necessary to move from our store front building to another location. We used every dollar we had for a down payment on the property. When the remaining amount was due, we still lacked 12,000 dollars. To keep from losing the property, Herschel wrote the check in faith and asked that it be held until closing. I heard him praying, "I've stepped out on the water and it feels like I'm going under for the third time. God, are you aware of the time?" The phone rang. A man we had never met was interested in investing in the project. He drove for four hours, picked up a check for $12,000 and deposited the exact amount we needed right on time. That is amazing!!!

Everything God called Herschel to do required a step of faith. By the time we began building the new church in Canton, Ohio on 38th Street, we had seen so many miracles, the word "impossible" no longer existed in our vocabulary. God could do anything! The building would be 50,400 square feet with a 1200 seat auditorium. We began the project without a dollar in the building fund.

God spoke to Herschel in a dream, "If you have to start digging the foundation with a spoon, start digging! I don't fill ditches until you dig them." The acquisition of the property was a miracle in itself. We made a down payment on the initial five acres. The owner gave us a clear title with no lien against the mortgage and carried the balance with monthly installments for three years.

During the site work, we needed fill dirt to bring our ground up to building level. There was a high hill on the property next door. We had the option to purchase those acres under the same contract. Jesus declared, "If you have faith as a mustard seed, you will say to this mountain, 'Move from here to there,' and it will move and nothing will be impossible for you," Matthew 17:20. Every time Herschel passed that land, he told the mountain to move. The plan of God was already in motion!

We didn't have the finances to have it excavated. We needed a miracle. A company contacted him and agreed, not only to pay a substantial amount of money for dirt, but did all of the excavation for our project as well. The dirt removal exposed a top grade vein of sand and gravel. We used it for our preparation work before we poured the concrete floors. The rest provided the base substance for the parking lot. We were blessed to purchase the remaining twelve and one half acres five years later. The owner gave us half the land and sold us the remaining acres for half price. Unbelievable!

Since we didn't own assets, the banks refused to give us a loan. It was a blessing in disguise. The interest rates were twenty-two percent. Our nation was suffering from a serious economic recession. Unemployment in Stark County was twenty-four percent. God had a plan. Our project and dilemma hit the news media. The church was built with seventy-five percent volunteer labor. Every time we needed workers with experience and expertise, skilled carpenters, electricians, plumbers, roofers, and laborers appeared on the construction site. It was the mildest winter on record and the men worked six days a week.

During the construction, three hundred thousand dollars were donated for materials. Often, when the bills for debts arrived, the words "no charge" were written on them. Eight hundred thousand dollars in financial loans came in from people throughout the community. Banks were suddenly interested in loaning us money. By the time the building was completed, every dollar in loans was paid back and every person who volunteered their services was called back to work.

Four Bibles were placed in the foundation with the prayer that from this church, the Word of God would go forth into all nations...and it has! An altar was built on the premises. Worship music was played around the clock. We had constant prayer for the protection of our workers.

On one occasion, a man and his son were on the roof preparing to nail shingles. The son was too close to the edge. When he inadvertently moved backwards, he stepped completely off the roof. His dad saw him falling but he was beyond his reach. Instantly, an invisible force pushed him up and forward until his dad was able to grab his hand and pull him back on the roof. How could that happen? One answer. Only God!

After building the frames for the walls, they were stood upright and hammered into position. When the carpenter swung the sledgehammer, it missed the wood and hit the man holding it on the other side in the forehead. His head was split open and blood was gushing out. He was in a daze.

They rushed him to the emergency room. While he was lying in the hospital bed, a miracle began happening before their eyes. The hemorrhaging stopped. It was amazing. The wound completely closed up without the need of stitches. He was dismissed from the hospital and back on the job site that afternoon. The medical staff was in awe. He didn't even have a headache.

One day in the upper corner of the rafters, a cloud began forming. At first, the construction crew was alarmed, thinking it was smoke. It was like a fog of heavy mist. The vapor completely filled the auditorium. There was such an awesome presence of God that the men fell on their knees. Some were lying prostrate on the floor and prayed for hours. It was such a profound experience that several of the construction workers became believers in God and the Christian faith for the first time.

It reminded us of a story in 2 Chronicles 5:13-14. While the trumpeters and singers were praising and thanking God, a cloud filled the temple. The priests could not stand to minister for the glory of the Lord had filled the house of God! My husband had a large sign placed outside our building site proclaiming: "To God be the glory!"

These statements were made repeatedly by those who walked through our doors: "This story has to be told! It is a modern day miracle!" One woman said that she had a dream of opening a day care center called "Grandma's House." It would have a rocking chair and the same loving care children receive in grandma's family room. After investing all of her savings she was closed down because of some technicalities.

The struggle was intense and her determination began to weaken. She was ready to forget the idea and accept defeat. Remembering the Cathedral of Life miracles on 38th Street gave her the courage to try again. She refused to give up. We watched her dream come true! She even began dreaming of expanding her idea into other cities. Only believe. God answers our prayers.

It is my prayer that the story of the "Miracle on 38th Street" will give every reader the faith and the courage to hold on to their dreams. The church stands as a reminder that with God, nothing is impossible. God is trustworthy. You can trust Him with your dreams. Miracles, signs, and wonders happen when you believe.

Today, the Cathedral of Life and the Inn at Belden Village Assisted Living Center are worth millions of dollars. Both assignments appeared impossible, but faith declared, "I expect a miracle!" If God can perform a miracle on 38th Street, He can perform a miracle on your street. God knows where you are!

CHAPTER TWENTY ONE
THE GAMMILL HOUSE

My husband's father was an ordained pastor in Mississippi. Herschel was born in a parsonage. He grew up living in Sunday School classrooms and homes adjacent to the church. His family moved every four years. When I was two years old, my parents moved into a big two-story house where I lived until I was eighteen. It was important to us for our children to be a part of a neighborhood in their own home. It was an exciting day when the Gammill family walked through the doors of our first home.

When Herschel accepted the pastoral position in Canton, Ohio, he asked to purchase the church parsonage. Several years later, Herschel felt an urgency for us to move from that location. He asked God for direction and contacted a real estate agency to arrange tours to some houses that were available. The realtor sent us to an 'Open House' in a relatively new upscale housing development. The cost was way beyond our range financially but we drove around the neighborhood anyway, admiring all of the exquisite homes.

On the next street, a beautiful two story home with high columns and a wrought iron balcony on the front porch captured our attention. It had the southern charm of one of those stately homes on a Mississippi plantation. Herschel stopped the car, pointed, and exclaimed, "There it is! That's the Gammill House!!!" Dana said, "It's not for sale." His dad said, "You will see. It's the house!"

One day, the owner of the real estate company called. We had never met him but He had seen Herschel many times on his daily "Life in the Spirit" telecast. He had a house to show us that would be perfect for our family. To our surprise, it was "The Gammill House." The home had been repossessed by the bank. The realtor had a cash offer for the asking price, but wanted to give us the first option.

We had to sell our house before negotiating any new transaction, so he took our house on trade. We didn't even have enough money for a down payment. Can you believe the real estate owner personally loaned us the money with no interest? Unbelievable!!! His generosity was unparalleled. The Bible calls it "Divine Favor." Proverbs 12:2 says, "A good man obtains favor from the Lord." Because of the adverse circumstances, the house sold for thousands of dollars beneath what it was worth. We moved into our new home with built-in equity. It was amazing!

We had no idea that this financial miracle would, ultimately, save our lives. It was the week before Thanksgiving. On our scheduled moving date, the weather forecast showed an extreme drop in the temperature. Because of the forecasted sub-zero frigid conditions, we asked Herschel to reschedule the move for a later date. He was adamant! "God says we have to move now!"

During the night, the temperature dropped way below zero. The next morning, we received a call. When the real estate agent entered our former house it was filled with gas fumes. A gas line had broken in the night. We were told that if we had been there, we would never have known what happened. We would have died in our sleep. It was a Thanksgiving we will never forget. God miraculously spared our entire family that night, including the generations who had not been born.

After our grandson, Michael, graduated from Oral Roberts University, he was contemplating buying a home. One day, he took his grandfather, who has dementia, out for a drive. Herschel said, "It's time for you to buy a house." Michael was shocked. He asked, "Papa, what did you just say?" He smiled and said, "Sure is nice weather, isn't it?" Michael always respected his grandfather's wisdom and advice. He researched the market and discovered on the Internet, a silent auction. It was on the same street he had already toured a home.

It was time to purchase another "Gammill house." Michael got pre-approved for the loan and asked God for direction. In the final five minutes, he pushed the button to bid the amount he felt impressed to offer. Within seconds, he received a response, "You just bought a house!" He bought a lovely four bedroom home for forty percent under the amount it would have cost him to build. He moved into his new home with built-in equity.

When his sister, Allison, and her husband moved to town, they built a new house on the next street. They almost have the same back yard. Because it was the last lot available at the time, they were given a forty thousand dollar discount. Trusting God is amazing. We bring everything to God, and we bring God into everything. Our Heavenly Father cares about "everything" that concerns us and supplies "everything" we need.

When Herschel and I made the decision to move into a condo, our son purchased our house. It still feels like home to our family. Every year we spend Thanksgiving at the *"Gammill House."* This year we celebrated the day with Isabella, our first great grandchild, and baby Elizabeth will be arriving by December thirty-first. Our home tells the story of our lives. It showcases the people we love and the places we have been. Our home is the sanctuary where we first connect with God and each other. It is the place we find rest at the end of the day.

Whether your house is a cottage, or a castle, it is God's presence that turns it into a home. God cares about where you live. You can travel from coast to coast or to the distant lands across the sea, but "there is no place like home." Proverbs 3:5-6, says, "Trust in the Lord with all your heart; And lean not unto your own understanding; In all your ways acknowledge Him, And He shall direct your paths." What an incredible promise!

Our home is our place of refuge. It hides us from the storms. Prior to my parents buying the home where I grew up, everything they possessed was destroyed in a flood. God provided a new house on "C Street." My childhood home survived all the storms of time with memories that have lasted a lifetime. They lived there fifty two years.

Once a year, my brothers and sisters still return to our hometown in Kansas for a family reunion. I always drive by the old home place. One time I stopped and introduced myself to the family who lived there. I prayed for God to meet their needs with miracles like He did for my family.

God has prepared mansions unlike anything this world has to offer. One day we will join the family of God for a "Welcome Home" celebration with our Heavenly Father. Your reservation is made the moment you accept His Son, Jesus Christ, as your Lord and Savior. He knows where you are!

"My people shall dwell in a peaceful habitation. In secure dwellings and in quiet resting places."

-Isaiah 32:18

"He who dwells in the secret place of the Most High, Shall abide under the shadow of the Almighty."

-Psalm 91:1

CHAPTER TWENTY TWO
THE INN

One of the dreams God placed in my husband's heart, was to build a nursing home. He always wanted to minister to the needs of people from the "Cradle to the Coronation." Twenty six years later, his dream came true. He founded and built the Inn at Belden Village, located on the very ground that once was a hill as high as the church. It is a part of our Cathedral of Life Ministries. The Inn is a beautiful, "state of the art," premiere Assisted Living Center with a wing for Special Memory Care. Its 101 suites accommodates 116 residents, depending on the style and size of the unit.

Our motto is, *"Celebrate your Life in Style."* The Inn has elegant dining rooms, and gathering rooms featuring comfortable lounges, a library with a pool table, a tea room, a bistro coffee shop, and a sports area with games. It offers a beauty shop, massage spa, and workout room with exercise equipment. It has its own beautiful theater, chapel, and Hub for stimulating activities, concerts and events. The computerized Samick Grand Player Piano, and the intercom music and sound system, creates a peaceful, relaxing atmosphere. There are fireplaces and large screen televisions throughout the building. The beautiful landscaping has lovely courtyards and outdoor picnic sitting areas with fountains and a waterfall.

During the construction of the building Herschel told God there was room for Him in the Inn. He prayed in every room for God to fill it so full of His presence that no one would ever feel alone. He prayed that each resident placed in our care would have a personal encounter with the love of God and the Lord Jesus Christ.

We have prayer and devotions every morning. We offer opportunities for weekly Bible studies and church services in our beautiful chapel. We prayed that God would send employees with compassion and love for those He placed in our care. We had no idea that the place Herschel was building to provide care for others, would one day provide the same care for him.

Herschel's prognosis gave us a greater personal understanding of the effects of the disease on not only the patient, but the entire family. He had been injured in an accident en-route to a speaking engagement. The doctor in the ER examined his broken ribs but was unaware he had hit his head. He started experiencing confusion, memory loss, and difficulty communicating. When we had his hearing tested, the hearing aids revealed that his brain was not sending signals and interpreting data properly. At first, the tests were inconclusive. The diagnosis was a mild cognitive impairment. Finally, two MRI tests and a PET Scan, showed hemorrhaging in the frontal lobe of his brain. The incurable damage appeared to have been caused from an aneurysm resulting from the injury.

I was standing in the produce department at the grocery store when my cell phone rang. As I heard the voice informing me of the final report from Herschel's test results, my whole body felt numb for a moment. The shock was traumatic. I looked down and lying beside the fruit, was a *"Jesus Calling"* book. I opened it and it seemed like the words from Isaiah 26:3 almost leaped off the page. God promised that "He will keep those in perfect peace whose mind is stayed on Him." It was a Word from God for the days to come.

When I took the book to the front counter, the clerk said, "We don't sell this book." I returned it to where I found it, and prayed that it would minister to someone else who was also in need of encouragement. I was in awe that God arranged such an unusual way to speak peace to my heart and let me know He was there. His amazing love reaches every one of us... wherever we are and He is always on time.

When we no longer had the ability to keep him safe, we moved Herschel into the Inn. We made his suite look like his office. We placed on the brass nameplate, Dr. C. Herschel Gammill. At first, he spent hours underlining scriptures and copying the words on paper as if he was writing another book. He always kept his Bible within reach.

One day, I was sitting in my car asking God, "Is his ministry over?" Instantly, the answers came. Was the ministry of the Son of God over when He came to earth and became like us? Is Herschel's ministry over because he left the corporate offices and went to the special memory care unit and became like one of them? In lucid moments, he treats the residents with compassion as if they are his congregation. God said, in Isaiah 55:9, "For as the heavens are higher than the earth, So are My ways higher than your ways, And My thoughts than your thoughts." I can give thanks to God for the things I don't understand because I know I can trust Him!

Herschel was often referred to as "a walking concordance." He could quote whole books of the Bible. He believed God for miracles and God performed them before our eyes; the blind could see; the deaf could hear, and people who were in wheel chairs got up and walked. We witnessed three people who had been pronounced dead restored to life. Nothing is impossible with God.

Although, Herschel can no longer communicate with us on a conversational level, he is often seen praying for those in our Memory Care. I don't know if God will heal him today or someday. I only know that just as God put it in Herschel's heart to prepare a place called, "The Inn," that would provide care for his every need; Jesus Christ has prepared a place called, "Heaven" to provide for him for all eternity! In other words, don't worry. Your present and your future are both secure. He knows where you are!

"Thou wilt keep him in perfect peace,
whose mind is stayed on Thee:
because he trusts in Thee.
Trust in the Lord forever: for in the Lord
Jehovah is everlasting strength."
-Isaiah 26:3 KJV

CHAPTER TWENTY THREE
THE ROBIN

It was our very first spring season in the Gammill House. On the ledge of one of the high columns on the front porch, my husband noticed we had acquired a tenant. A robin had dared to build a nest. Knowing the mess it was going to create on the porch below, Herschel asked the children to go out on the balcony and remove it from the ledge. We didn't realize that the bird lived there first, and the Gammill family were actually the intruders.

The little robin rebuilt the nest. The sixth time they knocked it down, little blue eggs fell and broke on the concrete beneath. The robin went out into the street and walked back and forth making a terrible screeching sound. It dive-bombed the windows of our house with its bill and began rebuilding the nest for the seventh time. I was reminded of the scripture in Proverbs, 24:16, "For a righteous man may fall seven times, And rise again."

This time, we watched as the mother sat, waiting for three more little blue eggs to hatch. We even saw the arrival of the baby robins as their shells broke open one at a time. We saw the mother bird search for food and return with their meals. Every day we listened to their songs.

One day, it was time and the mother scooted them out of the nest. They spread their little wings and began to fly. On Sunday, my husband's message was entitled, *"The Robin Who Wouldn't Give Up."* Through the years, in tough situations, when we were tempted to give up, we remembered the lesson the robin taught the Gammill family.

We all go through tough experiences in which it would be easier to say, "Forget it! I quit!" Instead, determination to succeed rises up with an "I can make it attitude" that refuses to give up. The story is told that Winston Churchill walked up to the podium at a graduation commencement service, spoke only three words, and returned to his seat. These unforgettable words were: *"Never Give Up!"* It became one of the most famous speeches ever given. Some stories are too personal and painful to share, but we all have memories of impossibilities that later became testimonies of triumph because we refused to give up.

Only two weeks ago, I wrote the story about the miraculous construction of our church on 38th Street. At 5:00 a.m. today I was writing the final paragraphs in the story of the Twin Towers. Later that morning, I was holding my iPad to read to my daughter: *"Picture everything you possess laying in a pile of ashes. If all you have left is your faith in God, you have everything you need"*... when the phone rang. Deana exclaimed, "The church is on fire!" She had just told me she woke up thinking, "The transition will be seamless." She discovered that the word, seamless, is defined as smooth, without interruption... But what transition???

While Dana and Deana were in shock, watching the smoke and flames pour out of the building, they suddenly understood that *those words* were a promise from God. We are so thankful that the building is still standing and no one was hurt. Easter Sunday is just around the corner and our grandson's wedding is happening in four weeks. It is undetermined how long it will take for the massive restoration, but "God has a plan."

I went to see my husband in the Special Memory Care of our Assisted Living Center adjacent to the church. He was quietly eating his breakfast, not a care in the world. He was giving me a picture of the peace God has available for me. I remembered how he never gave up during the construction of the building. When there was no money, he had asked the people to lay their hands on the wall frames and ask God for provision. The next week multiple truck-loads of dry wall appeared on the property with no charge. The company even sent its employees to install it professionally.

The fire was still not under control, but I had an unexplainable peace. I was working at the Inn directing activities that morning. I went about my business not knowing if the church would still be there when I finished my shift. The building was surrounded with fire trucks from three districts who didn't give up. They put their lives at risk and saved our building.

The east side of the church building suffered the most damage. In fact, the only thing that was not destroyed by either fire, smoke, or water was a small portion of drywall which had a Scripture attached. The Scripture in Romans 8:28 said, "And we know that all things work together for good to those who love God, to those who are the called according to His purpose."

Someone asked my son, "How is your church?" Dana answered, "Great!" The man said, "I heard on the news, it is on fire." He replied, "I thought you were talking about the church. The building is on fire, but the church is great!" Jesus said, ... "On this rock I will build My church, and the gates of Hell shall not prevail against it," Matthew 16:18.

It reminds me of another story. God sent His Son to the rescue. Jesus Christ gave His life on the cross to save us from death, hell, and the grave. On the third day, He arose. Jesus got up! He is alive! I've been to the tomb. It is empty!

This year the church will gather in a temporary place on Easter Sunday to celebrate His glorious resurrection. My son proclaimed in his sermon, "The Resurrection offers unlimited tomorrows. Because Jesus lives, you and I can face today and every tomorrow. We need another miracle on 38th Street. God did it once, and He can do it again! Every miracle increases our faith to believe again."

If you need a miracle today, don't give up! While God walked into that building with the firemen, He was giving me the peace to trust Him as I went to my job at the Inn. While He is taking care of us, He is even watching over the little sparrows and the robins!

Can you imagine how much He cares about you? You can make a decision like the little "Robin." Refuse to give up. Make this declaration of your faith, "God, I believe in You and I believe in miracles!!!" He knows where you are!

Let's pray together:

"Our Father which art in Heaven,
Hallowed be Your name.
Your kingdom come, Your will be done
On earth as it is in Heaven..."
-The Lord's Prayer
-Matthew 6: 9,10

CHAPTER TWENTY FOUR
THE WAKE UP CALL

Alarm clocks can be so irritating. It is disturbing when we are resting peacefully, and suddenly, without warning, a loud blast of noise interrupts our sleep. At least the snooze button gives us five more minutes to pretend it isn't time to get up. Sometimes in life, we get an unsettling wake up call that brings us into a shocking reality that is awakening our time-consciousness and forcing us to think beyond an inconceivable moment.

On the morning of September 11, 2001, our world came to a screeching halt. A nation that had forced prayer out of our schools was brought to its knees. The whole world watched in horror as the images and words flashed across our television screens, "The United States of America is Under a Terrorist Attack." At 8:45 a.m. Eastern Standard Time, a passenger plane crashed into the North Tower of the World Trade Center in Manhattan, N.Y. It was engulfed in enormous flames and black smoke. At 9:14 a.m., another plane crashed into the South Tower Both planes had been hijacked by terrorists on suicide missions.

Minutes later, another newsflash reported that the Pentagon in Washington D.C. had also been hit. Both of the former Twin Towers were like blazing infernos. We saw both of the massive structures collapse and disappear into twenty stories of ash and debris.

The night before 911, our daughter flew to lower Manhattan to visit a friend, and our son flew to D.C. for a meeting the next morning in the Capitol Building. I was finally able to contact Deana. She was in shock watching the events from just a few blocks away. Her cab driver had advised her to go to the top of the World Trade Center before 9:00 a.m if she planned to take pictures because heavy clouds were in the forecast. Deana prays every morning. She had no idea of the impact of that one decision, when she decided to wait. Thank God!

On my way to the church to pray, the news on my radio reported that a fourth plane was heading for the Capital. How could both of my children just happen to be in both of these dangerous places at this exact time? I was terrified. Dana reminded me that he was on a Divine Assignment. He joined an elderly African American woman walking around the capital, praying. She said, "Pray against bin la tin." Neither of them knew what those syllables meant. It later became evident that Osama bin Laden was the head of the terrorist organization who plotted and ordered the dastardly attacks.

Dana wrote in his weekly newspaper column, "On Tuesday morning of 911, I was in the U.S. Capital, praying. Todd Beamer was on the plane that had been commandeered by terrorists to crash into the Capitol Building. When Todd yelled, 'Let's roll,' he and the others on that flight became heroes, as they rushed their hijackers causing the plane to crash into a field in Pennsylvania. Their heroic action possibly saved hundreds of lives, including my own." Nearly three thousand people died, including the *Firefighters* and the *Policemen*, who courageously entered those burning buildings in an effort to save hundreds of precious lives. The devastation and heartbreak was unimaginable.

Since all flights were cancelled, we sent a van to to D.C. and N.Y.C. to bring them home. Deana had visited David Wilkerson's Time Square Church in Manhattan to inquire about what she could do to help. They ended up staying all week. The entire city was traumatized. The world as we had known it would never be the same. The sudden shock of this tragic catastrophe was felt in nations around the globe.

There were incredible stories of people who were supposed to have been there but were either late, or for unexpected reasons, unable to go to work that morning. There were those in shock who were distraught over their family members who were missing. People were suffering from inconsolable grief over the senseless deaths from the disastrous, unforgettable tragedy. Some families didn't get to say, "Goodbye or I love you," that morning. Only God can heal this kind of pain. Psalm 86:15 says, "But You, O Lord, are a God full of compassion and gracious." God can anesthetize and heal the places in our heart that medicine cannot reach. Our world is hurting. We have an opportunity to share our faith and watch God heal this nation.

In times like these we can't just change the subject and pretend it didn't happen. The clock is ticking. Listen to the wake up call. Get up! Our world has been summoned into a war between good and evil, and we don't even know where the enemy is or where to expect the next strike. The enemy knew the structure of the buildings. He planned and plotted his strategy. He knew when to strike in order to bring about the greatest devastation. The terrorists targeted and hit the exact place that was most vulnerable, weakening the structures. In minutes, they crumbled before our eyes.

It's strange that with all our sophisticated military and nuclear capability to protect our borders, we were helpless against the attack. It is ironic that the enemy was trained in the USA and used our own airplanes to destroy us. The picture of two of the greatest towers in the world exploding, falling, and plummeting into a pile of powder and rubble is indelibly imprinted into our hearts and minds.

There is another message in the picture. Jesus told a parable about two men in Matthew 7:24-27. The wise man built his house upon the rock. When the rain fell, the floods came, and the strong winds blew, the house was still standing. The foolish man built his house on the sand and when the storms came, it fell and crashed to the ground. The question is, "On what foundation are you building your life?" Don't be deceived!!! Be aware of the places that you are most vulnerable. How many people see their own lives crumble physically or spiritually because of bad choices?

In this anti-God war between the forces of good and evil it is time for us to declare, both as a nation and individually, which side we are on. Picture in your mind everything you possess lying in a pile of ashes. *If all you have left is your faith in God, you still have everything you need.* It is time to return to the Godly principles and values in which our country was founded. This part of history is being rewritten in our textbooks. It is time for the laws to be reversed denying the mention of God, and the rights of children to pray in our schools.

The following Sunday, churches all across America were filled with people praying. Only God can heal the brokenness in this nation. The answer to hate is love. Although, we don't live in a perfect world, we have a perfect Heavenly Father and a perfect Savior. God can take the shattered pieces of our lives and put them back together again. The final words spoken by my father were, "If My people who are called by My name will humble themselves, and pray and seek My face, and turn from their wicked ways, then I will hear from heaven, and will forgive their sin and will heal their land," 2 Chronicles 7:14.

What time is it? It is time to "Wake up America!" It is time to pledge our allegiance to this country once again and to the Republic for which it stands. We are still, "One nation, under God, indivisible, with liberty and justice for all," and "In God we trust." What time is it? It is time to pray!!! God hears and He answers our prayers. "God bless America and God bless those who bless America." He knows where you are.

CHAPTER TWENTY FIVE
THE ASSIGNMENT

The phone rang. The voice on the other end of the line asked if I was Gail Gammill. He said, "God told me to ask you to speak at a conference at my church." The pastor introduced himself and gave the date, the address, and the name of his church. I explained, "I am the pastor's wife. I'm sure you meant to call my husband or my son or daughter. They are the preachers of the family." He assured me that God said, "Gail Gammill."

He explained that I would not only be the first woman to speak at his church, but I would be the first white person to stand behind his pulpit. He stated that God told him I had a message for his church. My assignment would set the tone for the conference in the opening sermon. Of course, I said, "I'll be there." The word, "No" doesn't exist in my vocabulary. I hung up the phone thinking, "Really? Are you kidding me?" I teach children and Bible studies. I am a manuscript speaker. I know in advance what I'm going to say. I couldn't choose my favorite subject. I needed a message from God. Is that exciting, or what? I couldn't wait to see what God was going to say.

I knew it was a Divine appointment. Every night, before bedtime, I asked God to speak the message into my heart. Writing it down was the easy part. Nothing happened! So I set my alarm and woke myself up. I waited with my pen and paper, but still nothing happened! On the morning of the speaking engagement, I told my husband, "I have no idea what I'm going to say."

When I arrived at the church, I was escorted to a back room. They didn't bring me out until it was time to speak. Suddenly, I knew that God didn't have to wake me up and speak to me in the middle of the night. He could impart the words into my spirit and all I have to do is begin to speak. The only thing I had was a soundtrack of a song. The lyrics of the chorus were, *"When God's children love each other until their hearts become as one... Whenever we agree together, He promised He will be there and the work will be done."*

There is power in agreement! I can't remember what I said that day. It bypassed my brain and came from my spirit. I know that I quoted the words: "United we stand and divided we fall." I addressed those things that bring division and brought our focus on the values and beliefs which unites and consequently propels us into that place where nothing is impossible. Genesis 11:6 declares when people become unified as one voice, nothing they purpose to do will be withheld from them.

When our church caught on fire, there was no way to estimate a timetable for the restoration to be completed. We don't know when the doors on the 38th Street church will be re-opened. Sixteen years ago, my son had a dream that didn't make sense. He saw the Cathedral of Life meeting in a church on 31st Street. He never forgot the dream. Since then, that congregation moved and rebuilt their sanctuary in another location. The building was sold to the same church in which I spoke so many years ago. Their pastor became very ill and lost the ability to maintain their financial commitment. Consequently, the bank loan was foreclosed and the building had sat empty for over four years.

We purchased that property for a fraction of the original cost. While the Cathedral of Life building is being restored, we are restoring that church building. Once again, it will become a lighthouse in that neighborhood. During the interim period the auditorium can house our congregation with space for multiple midweek services, and special events, funerals, weddings, and an office facility.

A church in need of a building will be using the small chapel for their Sunday morning services. Another church meets in the main sanctuary on Sunday afternoons and Friday evenings. We also have a building that houses an educational facility for the Impact Academy which provides training for students with special needs.

Drug paraphernalia has been cleaned up from the grounds. A rock had been thrown through one of the sanctuary windows. Someone cleaning up the broken glass brought the rock to my son. Dana looked at the stone and said, "You know what this is don't you? I am holding in my hand a cry for help." I believe God heard that desperate cry.

It is very strange. If it hadn't been for the fire, we wouldn't have even considered buying a church building on 31st. Street, just a few streets away. It is providing us with another campus, giving us opportunities to minister to the needs in another community. A dark abandoned building is being restored into a place called, "Hope," illuminated with the love of God.

The church is not a building. The building is only the place we meet for corporate worship. We are now a church in motion. We announce every week where we will be meeting. It will never again be "business as usual." We are taking the message of Christ to the streets. We look for opportunities to witness. The assignment may be in the park, a cafe or coffee shop, at the mall… anywhere there is people. The Bible states in Isaiah 61:1-2, that God has commissioned and anointed us to preach the Gospel to the poor, to heal the broken hearted, to set the captives free, and to comfort and console those who mourn. It is time for the church of Jesus Christ to *"Be" the Church*!

The children passed out invitations to families in the community announcing special events. We are planning a summer Vacation Bible School and a Children's Festival this fall. We hope to offer a sports ministry in the gymnasium and special Saturday night miracle services in the sanctuary.

Some of the chapters in this book may not have even happened yet. What an adventure! It is so much fun waiting for the next story to unfold... waiting on the next assignment. I believe God can use the little spark that started the fire to ignite a flame that can create a wildfire in the spirit realm to spread the Gospel to the ends of the earth. It is remarkable the way God can turn a tragedy into triumph and bring good into every situation.

We are erecting a huge tent this summer on the 38th Street property. Many ministries throughout our region will be coming together to pray. We are believing for a Divine spiritual renewal in the state of Ohio. Our Ohio State motto is, *"With God, all things are possible."* After the fire, a teenager in our church built a stone Prayer Wall as an Eagle Scout project on our property. It is near the place we are planning to develop a community park. It stands as a memorial that God answers prayer. Over the wall the United States flag is flying in honor of our freedom to worship God. It is an open invitation for people to come and share their concerns with their Creator, and believe for miracles!

Our congregation has now been invited to emerge with the Trinity Gospel Temple. Many years ago, Pastor Dave Lombardi stepped out on faith and turned a shopping center into a church complex near downtown Canton. He and Meraline built a multi-faceted outreach with a Dream Center to feed and care for those in need, a campground for summer Youth Camps and Christian Retreats, and a world-wide television and radio ministry. We are excited about combining our ministries to reach our world with the Gospel of Jesus Christ.

Other ministries in our region are joining with us to see God multiply "His Church." Together, we are believing for a strategy to disciple millions of people for Christ. We hope someday to have our own Christian School and Bible College to teach, train, and unite generations of believers to fulfill *Christ's Great Commission* to heal our world.

We have an assignment to proclaim the infallible truth that Jesus Christ is the "only" answer! Acts 4:12 emphatically states, "Nor is there salvation in any other, for there is no other name under heaven given among men by which we must be saved." I believe a revival is being birthed that will return this nation back to its faith in God. A spiritual awakening with miracles, signs, and wonders is coming to planet Earth. In Joel 2:28, God promised that in the last days He will pour out His Spirit upon *all* flesh. He knows where you are.

CHAPTER TWENTY SIX
THE LAST MILE

Have you ever been traveling for hours and the mile marker on the highway is indicating that you are almost at your last mile...and then, "Oh no!" Another sign? "Road Work Ahead" and suddenly, "Road Closed" and a dead end. No way!

Have you ever run a race, and finally you can see flags waving and the crowd screaming, "You can make it?"... However, there are runners ahead of you and it's obvious you aren't going to get the trophy. It will only be the last mile if you choose to give up. There will always be another race. Stay physically fit, and keep heading toward the finish line at the next competition...

But what about those times when the detour sign doesn't provide an alternate route? Have you ever looked at your situation and couldn't remember purchasing the ticket for the trip? This place did not appear on my map or itinerary. How did I get to a town called "Nowhere?" Nowhere can end up in the place of despair, like the story of Chicken Little trying to keep the sky from falling.

Is God still in the drivers seat, or did I take the wheel and attempt to make it by myself? Did all of the "it's only one more thing" items on my-not-enough-hours-in-a-life-time, suck all of the oxygen out of my space? When you have exhausted all of your options and there is still too much month for the money; or too many problems and not enough answers; or the road you are traveling is leading to nowhere, it is time to re-calibrate.

The subsequent feeling of despair can produce hopelessness and hope is paramount for survival. So how do we get through those seasons when the heating and cooling system, the hot water tank, and the washing machine all stopped working the same week... and it's Christmas? You realize that you are wide awake. This is a nightmare, but you aren't sleeping. Then, what?

By the way, I've been there. There actually is a sign that says, "Nowhere, Arizona, Population: 0." We laughed, and took family pictures beside it for our vacation album. No wonder the population was zero. It is only a mirage. You can't stay there! You have to re-focus. For me, it starts with dismissing anxious thoughts by placing my trust in God. He is my strength and help in times of drought. He always provides a way through the desert places in life. If I want to enjoy the journey, I have to command my attitude to adjust to the hopefully temporary, new difficult circumstances.

One thing I have discovered is that wherever God leads, there will be adventure. The exciting part about the last mile is arriving at our destination or returning safely to that place we call "Home." The hard part is those miles between the unexpected obstacles and valleys we go through. Distractions are designed to cause us to lose momentum. The secret is trusting God even when we can't see where the next mile will take us. It is committing to *His* will and *His* way.

I visited the Garden of Gethsemane where Jesus was almost at the last mile on His way to the Cross. I cannot even imagine the agony He was feeling. He knew in advance what He was facing when He prayed these Words, "Not my will, but thine be done!" He modeled for us that the way of the Cross leads home. Only those who understand total surrender will make it victoriously to that last mile of their purpose and destiny. Your only job is to follow where He leads.

When I was a child, I was always the first one in the car. I remember dad cancelling a trip because we didn't have gas money. I reminded him that Jesus turned water into wine. I was confident if he would let me pour water into the gas tank, it would turn into gas. Dad decided, "When God turns it into gas in the gas can, I will pour it into the tank." Good choice. Wisdom is a necessity!

As a child I will never forget traveling through the hot desert en-route to New Mexico for miles with the gas gauge flashing below the letter, "E." Every gas station was closed. My dad prayed for God to cause our car to run on empty and it did! We drove all night with no gas. Instead of the last mile leaving us stranded on the road, we arrived at our destination. God answered our prayer.

One time my car was registering below empty. I was running late to a funeral home. It was dark when I left the calling hours and pulled into a gas station. Two weird looking guys pulled up in a van and started walking towards my car. I locked my door. No one else was around, so I left with no fuel. An amazing thing began to happen. I literally watched the gauge go from empty to full as if I had pumped gas. I drove my car for three weeks and the gas gauge stayed on full. It was incredible!

It's exciting to remember the great miracles, but what about those times when you're stuck in a situation, and there is no miracle in sight? Dana and his roommate were driving all night returning to the Oral Roberts University campus in Tulsa, Oklahoma. About ninety miles past Saint Louis, the car started making a loud noise and came to a complete stop. The ignition wasn't responding to fire-up the engine. Dana noticed a textbook in the car written by Oral Roberts. His picture was on the cover and the words, "Nothing is impossible."

Dana told Lee to lay the book on the engine as a point of contact with his faith. He would try again to start the engine and believe for a miracle. Lee said, "If it happens, I'll eat my hat." Guess what! It happened! The car functioned perfectly all the way for over three hundred miles. The second they rolled onto the ORU campus, the car made a sputtering noise, stopped, and that was its last mile. Lee didn't eat his hat, but it was a miracle never forgotten.

This year, my son had asked our congregation to reduce our New Year's Resolutions to one word. His word was, "Simplify." Within five months, our church caught on fire; the gas well on the property developed a leak saturating the land on which we we had planned the construction of a Community Park behind the church this summer; a main city water-line broke and flooded the property with water; and when we erected a tent, the wind caused part of it to collapse. In the meantime, we were faced with the dilemma of relocating our congregation to a new location.

While all this trauma was happening, my husband started having seizures and requiring specialized care twenty four hours a day. Simplify all that! I watched the stress begin taking its toll on every member of my family; physically, emotionally, and financially. So what do you do the day before the miracle? It was time to put our faith to the test.

I remind myself of miracles I have experienced or read about in the Bible. Hope arrives in stories like the three Hebrew boys being thrown into the fiery furnace because they wouldn't deny their faith in God. The heat was turned up seven times hotter. A fourth man, the Son of God, appeared in the fire and they walked out unharmed. The men who cast them into the fire didn't survive the heat.

The disciples survived the storm on the Sea of Galilee and made it safely to the other side. Jesus simply spoke, and the wind obeyed. The storm was over! It may seem like the last mile when you are going through the fire, or sinking under the waves of the storms of life, but God always has a plan with a way out!

Some miracles are dependent on our own choices. Dana was in the lead car of a caravan of vehicles transporting a large group of teenagers to a theme park. Suddenly, he felt impressed to pull off the highway. The others followed him and waited for several minutes until he felt released to continue the trip. Shortly after they got back on the road, they realized they had avoided being in a pile-up of several cars in a horrendous accident. They arrived in time to pray and give comfort until the emergency vehicles could arrive. It pays to listen to the voice of God. It may be a gentle nudge in your inner spirit, but being sensitive to God-given intuition can save your life.

Life is invariably filled with defining moments of decision and opportunities that chart the course of destiny. I remember the feeling of holding each of my babies for the first time in awe of the miracle of life. Knowing they were beginning their "first mile" was a sobering moment. The realization of my responsibility as a role model in each mile of their journey was overwhelming.

The Bible is our infallible instruction manual. The Holy Spirit is our teacher and tour guide. The journey is about the manner in which we choose to live our life. Our decisions will determine the direction we are heading. Will the path you are on lead to consequences and remorse or to purpose and destiny? My grandson, Blake, stated on his Facebook page: "Change begins with a choice and that continues with commitment. To change your direction you have to change your actions."... "Let the words of my mouth and the meditation of my heart be acceptable in Your sight, Oh Lord, my strength and my redeemer," Psalm 19:14.

The Apostle Paul said in Hebrews 12:1 ..."Let us run with endurance the race that is set before us, looking unto Jesus, the author and finisher of our faith." Jesus promised in Revelation 22:12, "And behold I am coming quickly, and My reward is with Me to give to every one according to his work." Finish the race! He will be there when you cross the finish line.

I just woke up. It is 4:00 a.m. again. Last week someone asked me, "What is today?" I knew they were expecting the date. My answer was, "It is today." I knew it wasn't yesterday and it wasn't tomorrow yet. It felt as if time was standing still and I was locked temporarily into the moment.

These past two days our family sat around the bedside of my husband knowing that each breath could be his last. The peace of God filled the room. We sang together, we laughed together, we cried together, and we prayed together. My husband always taught us that we can worship our way through anything.

Wow! I just realized something. There is no last mile on this trip! There is only a *next* mile. Soon my husband will take a journey from time into eternity. He is going "Home." We can't go with him, but he won't go alone. Herschel will leave the land of the dying and be escorted into the land of the living.

His miracle will happen the moment he breathes the celestial air of that Holy City. His pain will evaporate into the bliss of a celebration like no other. Time will be no more. The "next" mile will last forever. One day, each of us will arrive in that place of endless tomorrows. Rejoice through every mile of your journey. Have a great trip! God has a plan and He knows where you are.

...Tonight Herschel took his trip of a lifetime. His arrival time was scheduled for 10:20 p.m. and he arrived on time. Destination: Heaven. I can almost hear his voice shouting, "The eagle has landed." He's home! "But as it is written: Eye has not seen, nor ear heard, Nor have entered into the heart of man the things which God has prepared for those who love Him," 1 Corinthians 2:9.

The disciples of Christ witnessed His crucifixion, burial, resurrection, and ascension into Heaven. In 2 Corinthians 5:8, the Apostle Paul tells us that when we are *absent* from the body, we are *present* with the Lord. We are a three-part being which is made up of a body, a soul, and a spirit.

The body is the house we live in. Herschel called it "the earth suit." The soul is made up of the mind, the will, and the emotions by which we relate to the world around us. The spirit is the Life within us from which we connect with our Father, God. It is recorded in Genesis 1:27, "So God created man in His own image..." God is eternal and the Life He created in us will live forever in eternity.

Herschel is already there. His earth suit is waiting it's glorious resurrection near that same airport from which he traveled the globe preaching the Gospel. I smiled as the planes flew over. I will see him at the next mile. Today I remind myself, "You are not alone. God knows where you are."

" Dear God, Grant me the serenity
to accept the things I cannot change;
To change the things I can;
And the wisdom to know the difference."
-Prayer of Serenity

Today
Whether I see the sun shine or not
I choose to be happy.
-Dana Gammill

CHAPTER TWENTY SEVEN
THE SIGN

When Herschel and I went on a road trip, it was never about enjoying the ride. It was always about arriving at our destination. When we stopped for gas, we took care of all of our business at the same time. We would pick up fast food or snacks and stay on the road.

We had been traveling for hours when a highway billboard caught my husband's attention. The sign was an irresistible advertisement for a restaurant in the next city. It was called the Prime Rib and you could almost smell the food cooking on the grill. I was surprised to hear the clicking sound of the turning signal at the next exit. He said, "We're stopping for a nice dinner."

The Prime Rib appeared to be a very expensive place. Are you kidding me? We looked like bums. I was surprised they let us in the door with our blue jeans and tennis shoes. A few minutes later, we were waiting to be served our entree when I noticed a lady, sitting alone. I said, "I think God wants me to go talk to her." She was quietly eating her meal. Herschel said, "Why don't we just pray for her." When we gave thanks for our meal, he included her in his prayer.

I started trying to talk myself out of it. "What if I upset her?" I couldn't eat. I realized this stop was not about the food. It was a Divine assignment. I knew had to speak to her. As the lady finished her meal, my heart started racing. When the waiter returned with her credit card and meal ticket, I knew in a moment she would be gone and it would be too late. While approaching her table, God was speaking into my heart; "Tell her I love her. I have plans for her future. She is not alone."

When I spoke those words, she was shocked. She seemed so sad. Tears came into her eyes and she said, "This was going to be my last meal. I was planning to go home, take a bottle of pills, and end my life. I thought it wouldn't matter. I didn't think anyone would care." She was contemplating a permanent solution for a temporary problem. I said, "I'm so sorry you are hurting, but God has a better plan." She smiled and said, "Thank you."

I believe the impact of that inevitable moment with destiny will be revealed in eternity. I was so grateful for the privilege to be used by God to deliver His message. I'm sure God would have sent someone else if I had not heard and obeyed His voice... His love always finds a way.

Can you imagine how much detail went into the planning of this Divine appointment? It was like one of those movies introducing two separate sets of characters. It is apparent that eventually they will connect, but you're trying to figure out how it will happen. God had to have her and us in the same place at the same time.

So Herschel and I ended up in a place we had never been before, and the hostess just happened to seat us in the same section? Really?... God's GPS orchestrated the entire event. I'm sure the people placing the sign in that exact spot, never dreamed it could save someone's life.

It isn't the first time God used a sign on the road. In the first Christmas story, He sent signs in the sky to announce the birth of His Son, who was born to save the world. A bright light and a host of angels appeared to the shepherds saying, "This will be the sign unto you. You will find a babe wrapped in swaddling cloths lying in a manger."

The wise men followed a star to the location of the Christ child with a warning to save His life. Jesus said in John 8:12, "I am the light of the world. He who follows Me shall not walk in darkness, but have the light of life." He not only lights our way, He is 'The Way.' Look for the signs He sends to direct your path. The Bible says, "The steps of a good man are ordered by the Lord,.." Psalm 37:23.

Signs come in many forms. Deana was crying as she drove down our street feeling the loss of her father the day before the funeral. Suddenly, white iridescent feathers and twenty dollar bills began falling on the hood and front window of her car. Her dad used to keep twenties in a separate place to give away. The bills were folded like he always methodically folded them. She pulled over. There was no wind and nothing above the car except the feathers and falling money. It was a gift from her Heavenly Father reminding her, "I am still here."

At the committal service our great-granddaughter picked up a white feather exactly like the others. There was only one. Everywhere we went, we saw rainbows and there was no rain in sight. One of the rainbows was a complete circle around a cloud at the very top of the sky. Rainbows are signs of God's promises. We received them as love notes reminding us that God is with us.

God uses all kinds of signs to get our attention. It has been a volatile season. Almost daily, every major news network is reporting "simultaneous" worldwide disasters and tragedies, earthquakes, hurricanes, floods, catastrophic wild fires, violent murders, and unprecedented massacre in the streets. We hear the sound of nuclear threats on the horizon. Renegade nations seeking to destroy the earth are creating fear and terror around the globe. In times like these, keep your trust in God.

It reminds me of when the disciples asked Jesus in Matthew 24:3-7,12 "...what will be the sign of Your coming, and of the end of the age?" He answered, "You will hear of wars and rumors of wars." He said, "For nations will rise against nations, and kingdoms against kingdoms, and there will be famines, pestilences, and earthquakes in various places." He warned that lawlessness will abound.

These prophecies are being fulfilled daily. Read Luke 21:7-36. It describes this generation. Jesus said in verse 28, "Now when these things begin to happen, look up and lift up your heads, because your redemption draws near."

During the forty days after Christ's death and resurrection, He spoke with His disciples of future events pertaining to the kingdom of God. His ascension is recorded in the book of Acts 1:9-11. "He was taken up into the heavens and a cloud received Him out of their sight." As they were gazing into the heavens, two angels appeared. They explained that Jesus will come again in the same manner as they had seen Him leave. This generation could see this come to pass.

The earth is in travail. A new dispensation is in the process of being birthed. This is our finest hour. God doesn't order the chaos, but He is in control of its final outcome. The signs of the times remind us that Jesus promised in Matthew 24:13-14, "But he who endures to the end *shall be saved*. And this gospel of the kingdom will be preached in all the world as a witness to all nations and then the end will come." God's plan is in motion. Get ready!

Last week my grandson, Michael, was standing in a hotel Starbucks line for coffee. A lady asked him why he was here. When he said, "I am attending a conference," she asked what it was about. He told her the previous night a woman was there from Uganda whose face had been left with scars from a violent assault. On the same stage was the man who attacked her. They spoke on forgiveness. The woman said, "I don't think I could forgive that." Michael told her, "Jesus Christ gives us the ability to forgive. Would you like to ask Him to help you?" She said, "I believe I would." She not only left with her coffee. She had a Word from God that could change her life.

You and I were placed in this generation for "such a time as this." The signs all around us only point us to our purpose on the earth. It is time to take the good news of *"Joy to the world, the Lord has come"* and defy hate with love; to find those who are hurting and bring hope; to speak blessings and truth in an age of deception. Make this declaration with me: "I was born for this moment!" Look up! Stand up! Speak up! God's GPS will guide you. Don't miss the signs He places in your path. He knows where you are.

CHAPTER TWENTY EIGHT
THE ANGELIC ENCOUNTERS

Our modern society is enamored and fascinated with angelic beings and supernatural power in the spirit realm. Colossians 1:16 says, "For by Him all things were created that are in heaven and that are on earth, visible and invisible, whether thrones, or dominions, or principalities or powers," Much of that which is viewed in the contemporary media is imaginary, but angels are real. They are sent by God on specific, supernatural missions.

Throughout the Bible you will see them make an appearance to deliver, guard, guide, comfort, and supply aid to those in need. They are immortal beings created by God with supernatural ability. They are not limited by gravity, time, or space. Unlike God, who is omnipresent, they can only be present in one place at a time. Their presence can be visible or invisible. Psalm 34:7 says, "The angel of the Lord encamps all around those who fear Him, And delivers them."

Throughout the years, our family has experienced some unforgettable encounters with angels. Most of them were accompanied with a miracle. I will share several of these supernatural manifestations in the next few paragraphs.

Years ago we were attending a church conference at the Memorial Auditorium. Some friends from New Orleans invited our ten year old son to see their bus that was parked across the street. When he returned, without looking, Dana ran back into the street right in front of an oncoming car going fifty miles an hour.

The memory of the sound of the brakes screeching and the impact that followed still makes my heart race. The car hit him and we saw him falling. It would have crushed him beneath the wheels, but something miraculous happened. It was as if an invisible force literally lifted him up, carried him horizontally thirty feet, and sat him down in a standing position.

Dana exclaimed, "It felt like something picked me up!" He didn't even have a bruise. The driver was crying and visibly shaken. She said, "When I hit him, I saw a big hand lift him from the front of my car." I can still see his new shirt flying through the air. I still have it in my closet. It was touched by an angel! The experience left us in a state of awe.

After graduating from high school, our children attended Oral Roberts University. One morning as they were leaving the campus, a car came over the hill traveling eighty miles per hour. The impact actually knocked Deana into the back seat. Her rings even flew off her fingers. Dana's head hit the front windshield. He was in a daze and bleeding profusely. He didn't remember yelling, "We have to get out!" Deana was pinned between the seats. If he hadn't moved across the front seat, got out, and pulled her from the back of the car, it would have been too late. He saved both of their lives. Within seconds, the car exploded like a bomb into flames and completely incinerated.

The City of Faith Hospital was located in view of the campus. A stranger dressed in white appeared, lifted, and literally carried both of them from the accident to the entrance of the emergency room... and then mysteriously disappeared. When they asked what happened to the person who helped them, they were told that they were alone. No one saw the third person.

One time, Dana and another student from ORU left the campus, driving all night to get home for Christmas. He became sleepy and the girl offered to drive. He woke up and the car was swerving all over the road. She had fallen asleep. From the passenger side of the car he grabbed the steering wheel, but the car was out of control.

All he could do was scream the name of Jesus. The car began rolling over an embankment, and then stopped abruptly before hitting a telephone pole. An angelic being intervened. There was no other explanation. It was miraculous!!!

Another time, Deana and I were driving back to Ohio from ORU. We were in heavy traffic. I was changing lanes and inadvertently pulled in front of a car in my blind spot. We were going at high rates of speed. When the car on the side of my vehicle swerved, we both lost the control of our automobiles. It caused a chain of reactions. It was terrifying. Cars were barely missing each other all over the highway. Finally, I was able to pull off the road. Everyone was safe!!! Deana was afraid to open her eyes. We couldn't believe it. There had to have been angels preventing all those cars from colliding in a horrific tragedy.

My granddaughter is married to a man named "Hunter." The story behind his name is amazing. His grandfather is a minister. He was flying his plane to a speaking engagement. While en-route it began having mechanical problems. The plane crashed into a remote forest area. He was lost for fifteen hours, surrounded by the wreckage, lying in his own blood beneath the log of a tree. He had multiple broken bones and internal injuries. A man dressed like a hunter told him to hold on. All night Charlie quoted, "I will live and not die."

The hunter led the emergency team to the crash site. When the rescue team couldn't remove the tree, the hunter yelled three times, "Oh my God!" And instantly, they watched the tree move and was mysteriously lifted into the air and removed. There had to have been other invisible angels on the scene. It was strange that the hunter standing beside them didn't show up in any of the pictures. Both deputy sheriffs became Christians.

The doctor did not expect him to survive the flight to the hospital. After numerous surgeries, he was told that he would never walk again. Isaiah 53:5, referring to Christ on the cross says, ..."And by His stripes we are healed." He received a miracle. He not only walks, he still flies a plane! The rescue team reported that when the hunter walked away, he disappeared before their eyes. When Hunter was born, his parents named him after the angel.

My mother had a phenomenal experience when she was a child. She was returning from the barn to the house and saw a celestial being on the gate. The angel had blond hair and was robed in a radiant, shimmering garment. She could hear her mother calling her, but was too shocked to move. Grandma witnessed the incident from the house. Moments later, the angel vanished into the air. One of mother's favorite verses was, "For He shall give His angels charge over you, To keep you in all your ways," Psalm 91:11.

The experience of seeing her guardian angel left an impact on her life that was never forgotten. In the moments prior to her death, the week of her ninetieth birthday, Mom described the encounter with the angel as if it happened yesterday.

My daughter encountered two guardian angels on the highway while driving through dangerous blizzard conditions. It was a complete whiteout as if the planet Earth had been turned upside down, producing a giant size snow globe. The road was almost solid ice. It was a frightening, very intense situation. Deana was desperately trying to keep the car from sliding off the road. As the ladies in the car were praying quietly for protection, they saw two forms facing them in the distance on the the road. These images were coming toward them, as if walking in synchronized movement.

As they moved closer, the scene appeared like a projected hologram image. As the angelic beings with long flowing hair, dressed in white glistening garments passed by, they became translucent and evaporated into the air. It was surreal. Instantly, they knew God had allowed angels to make their presence visible as they prepared the way for their safety. My husband and I had similar experiences while traveling in Mississippi and North Carolina. Angels are Heavenly beings authorized by God to engage in acts of supernatural warfare, assistance, and protection.

A woman in our church was given the report that her unborn baby had a serious heart condition, and she should consider abortion. Of course that was not an option. I invited her family to come to our home for a thanksgiving meal. We would give thanks and pray for God to heal the baby.

I've never had Thanksgiving without a turkey, but I thought it would be easier to serve a pre-cooked honey baked ham. I was at the counter paying for the ham, when a stranger came into the store and walked over to me. She said, "You're supposed to be buying a turkey." She turned and walked back out of the store. It was confirmation that a miracle was on its way. The incident increased our faith to believe. We knew God would be there! The baby girl survived the challenges with her heart issues. Today, she is a beautiful teenager.

The Bible tells us in Psalm 103:20 that angels listen and obey the voice of the Lord. Can you imagine what our world would be like if everyone listened to the voice of God? God speaks to us through nature. He speaks through the Holy Scriptures. He speaks to us in dreams and visions. He speaks to us by sending people or angels to speak words of wisdom and hope. Hebrews 13:2 advises, "Do not forget to entertain strangers, for by so doing, some have unwittingly entertained angels." Recognize God's voice when He sends unique messages and messengers. He knows where you are.

This prescription
cannot be bought in a bottle.
It is found only in God:

"But those who wait upon the Lord
Shall renew their strength;
They shall mount up with wings like eagles,
They shall run and not be weary,
They shall walk and not faint."
-Isaiah 40:31

CHAPTER TWENTY NINE
THE EAGLE

Traveling to Israel and getting to walk where Jesus walked was on my wish list for every member of my family. It was like a dream come true for my husband to take our son there when he was a young man. Our daughter had the privilege to host tours to the Holy Land for three years. It was one of the highlights of my life when she invited her dad and I on one of her trips.

Now, it was our grandson, Michael's turn. My son and I were visiting when his phone rang. Michael was calling from Jerusalem. He was so excited describing the events of his tour. The day before, someone on the street invited him and another tourist into a synagogue. It was daylight and the synagogue was close-by, so they followed him inside. Michael never wants to miss anything. His dad advised him that some places are not safe and to only stay with his own tour group.

The next day, our local TV news channel reported that a synagogue in Jerusalem had been invaded by terrorists and four Americans were murdered and hacked up with knives. Immediately, we were receiving calls from prayer partners inquiring if Michael was okay. Michael contacted his dad to let him know he was safe and thanked him for the warning. The incident had taken place in the same area where Michael was touring. The Bible says, "A man's heart plans his way, But the Lord directs his steps," Proverbs 16:9.

The safest place in the world is in the center of God's will. It is a place of Divine favor. The Bible says in Psalm 5:12, "For You, O Lord, will bless the righteous; With favor You will surround him as with a shield. Psalm 32:10, "...But he who trusts in the Lord, mercy shall surround him,"

When the tour ended, Michael was at an airport in Germany waiting for his next connection en-route home. The rest of the tour group had already left on their scheduled flights. The Bible says in Psalm 91:1,9-10, "He who dwells in the secret place of the Most High shall abide under the shadow of the Almighty... Because you have made the Lord, who is my refuge, Even the Most High, your dwelling place, No evil shall befall you."

Dana was at home praying and felt prompted to call and ask Michael, "Where is your passport?" He told his dad that it was right beside him in his carry-on bag. Instantly, Dana said, "Put it in your hand! Now!" Michael was shocked when he saw the woman sitting next to him had her hand in his carry-on luggage. He grabbed his bag and quickly examined the contents, relieved that his passport was still there.

While standing in the line to finally board the plane, he was approached by airport officials and taken to a holding room for questioning. They began searching his luggage and interrogating him. They bomb swabbed his hands, hair, and clothing to check for traces of explosives. Since he had already been cleared through security, he was aware that the scrutiny was not normal procedure. He didn't know if someone reported the incident or if something illegal could have been placed into his luggage. He had no idea what was going on. He was told he was being detained and was not allowed to leave the room.

Michael called his dad to explain what happened and inform him that he may miss his flight. They lost connection and the only information Dana had was that the flight had left. We would not know if he was on the plane until it arrived in the USA hours away. I said, "Well, God knows."

I walked to my kitchen window and saw a huge bird soaring across the lake toward my house. It flew right up to my window, turned, and headed back across the water. I ran for my camera and asked God to send it back. I was able to capture the eagle on film as it soared across the water repeating again the same performance, then flying away. When my husband traveled, he always called back when he reached his destination and said, "The eagle has landed." It is the only time I have ever seen an eagle where I live. But that day God sent an eagle to my house to say, "The eagle is in flight."

It is needless to say, the flight was on time and Michael was on board the plane! Thank God our angels travel with us. He was escorted to the plane with barely enough time as it was preparing to take off. He never knew what God prevented from happening. I keep the eagle picture on my kitchen counter to remind me that God knows where I live and He answers my prayers.

Jesus promised in Matthew 28:20, "...and lo, I am with you always, even to the end of the age." You can insert your name at the beginning of that verse. That promise is for "you." You are not alone. He knows exactly where you are!

CHAPTER THIRTY
THE ABUNDANT LIFE

How would you describe "Abundant Living"? My initial reaction was "happiness and contentment." When I heard that Walgreens claims that they are located on the corner of Happy and Healthy, I said, "I'm going straight to the health and happy aisle and buy all I can afford of each." Maybe I'll just sit on the corner of the parking lot and eat a McDonalds's "Happy Meal" until I have time to watch one of those "Happy Ever After" Hallmark movies. So now I am being ludicrous! There are times I need some comic relief.

Really? Between the evening shadows under the canopy of a dim, star-lit sky, and the days when the sun is hiding behind the clouds, there has to be some lasting happiness..."somewhere, out there." Everyone is looking for happiness and guaranteed satisfaction. Unfortunately, in life there are no real guarantees. Many billboards and advertisements are designed to mislead the public by offering a product that doesn't have the ability to produce what it promises. Their instant relief and instant answers don't always match the results.

Abundant living doesn't mean you will never have a problem. There is no perfect life, but you can have peace in the midst of conflict; joy in spite of circumstances; faith to believe for healing in times of sickness; mercy and favor where there is injustice; love and laughter even in a sick world that has been corrupted with hate and filled with sorrow. What a vast contrast, but it is not too good for it to be true. God's way of living life defies the world's system of thinking.

Jesus said in John 10:10, "The thief does not come except to steal, and to kill, and to destroy. I have come that they may have life, and that they may have it more abundantly!" Jesus has the ability to do what He says He will do. He is backed up by all of Heaven. He has at His command the hosts of warring and guardian angels.

It is so shocking when you discover something is missing and realize it was deliberately taken from you. One time when we returned home it was obvious that someone had broken into our house. Deana was delighted. She was running around the house playing detective with a magnifying glass, looking for finger prints. A pillow case, loaded with items from Dana's room was left on the floor by the back door. It appeared that someone had become frightened and left in a hurry. Can you imagine the look on the thief's face when our guardian angel showed up?

My son tells about waking up one morning and discovering that someone had broken into their garage. His brief case was missing from his car. It contained his Bible, wallet, a special ring, and his computer with hours of sermon material. On the way to school the children remembered the story of King David when everything he held dear was taken. They sang *"I went to the enemy's camp and I took back what he stole from me."* They prayed for a miracle and believed that it would be returned.

Life is about choices. Instead of letting it ruin his day, Dana made a decision to trust God to answer their prayer. He said, "This afternoon when we get home from school, there will be a surprise waiting for us." When they pulled into the driveway, the briefcase was sitting on the front porch. Nothing was missing. There was no explanation. It was an amazing portrayal of the abundant life Christ promised those who place their trust in Him.

It was our daughter's first trip to the Holy Land. The second day she was there, her wallet was stolen with all of her identification, credit cards, and cash from her purse. Fortunately, her passport was in a separate place, but she was facing the dilemma of being there with no money for ten more days. A minister from the Canary Islands prayed with her. He told her that he felt the wallet would be returned, but not until she was back home in America. "God would provide."

Deana had a choice to become anxious and fearful, or trust God in a situation that was beyond her control. It was amazing! Everywhere she went in the marketplace, meals, gifts, and supplies were given to her free of charge. A man walked up to her and placed five one hundred dollar bills in her hand. Every need was miraculously supplied by complete strangers or someone she had just met.

The week after she returned home, she received a letter from the United States Embassy in Athens, Greece. She had never traveled to Greece. They had her wallet. It was sent to her via express mail and not one thing was missing. The experience increased her faith in God to fulfill His promise to abundantly supply even *more* than enough. What a powerful illustration of the faithfulness of God on a daily basis.

Everyone has disconcerting moments which can potentially produce anxiety on some level. I have a magnet on my refrigerator door with a picture of John Wayne sitting on a horse and these words: "Courage is being scared to death, but saddling up anyway." The picture speaks volumes. Fear levels can range from anxiety to panic and terror.

While driving my husband to the airport for a three week trip to Africa, I was informed that I had to speak on his daily "live" radio programs. It was one of those "ready or not, here I come" experiences. At noon, every day, nervous or not, I was on the air. By the time he returned, I decided to continue having my own show one day a week.

In order to live life abundantly we have to face the challenges in life. We have to conquer the thieves that would rob us of living life to the fullest. What is robbing you of your joy? What is stealing your peace? What is keeping you from developing the full potential of your purpose and destiny? Is it fear? Is it uncontrolled anger? Is it bitterness?... In order to face the giants and lions in our life, we have to "run to the roar." We have to intentionally take authority over anything that prevents us from fulfilling God's perfect plan for our life.

When my daughter was young, she was attacked by bees while riding her bicycle. She developed an irrational fear. If a bee landed on the windshield, she literally would not get out of the car. One day, her dad brought his brief case into the study. It had been left in the garage for several days. When Deana opened his office door, bees were swarming around the room. She was terrified. She slammed the door, and called her dad, screaming.

One bee was still flying around the kitchen sink. She remembered that in Genesis 1:26, God gave us dominion over every living thing, even bees. She commanded it to cease intimidating her. It literally fell dead into the sink. When her dad arrived, he opened the study door and said, "There are no bees in here!" Deana ran into the room and bees were laying dead all over the floor. Her fear was dismantled. She was never afraid of bees again.

My aunt Mary Ann is so amazing. She is over one hundred years old and still lives a productive life. When asked her secret she said, "I don't worry about anything." Philippians 4:6-7, "Be anxious for nothing, but in *everything* by prayer and supplication, with thanksgiving, let your requests be made known to God; and the *peace of God* which surpasses all understanding will guard your hearts and minds through Christ Jesus." In other words: "Turn your worries into prayer."

Jesus brought us abundant living which takes us beyond the prosperity of the good times, to having the courage to face the struggles and financial reversals in the difficult times. Abundant living doesn't have room for unresolved conflict that can produce everything from uncontrolled anger, to living in fear, and depression.

Don't live beneath your privileges. Every minute you spend feeling angry or sad, you lose sixty seconds of happiness. Don't allow disappointment or worry to be placed in the driver's seat. If the thief leaves you feeling distressed, ask God for the courage to get up on the saddle. Give God the reigns. He knows where you are.

CHAPTER THIRTY ONE
THE BIG PICTURE

I remember the first time I flew on an airplane. Feeling the force of those big engines defying the force of gravity was exhilarating. Looking down at at the world from that distance made all of the objects below seem small and insignificant. It was amazing soaring through the clouds and seeing the brilliance of the sun still shining. So this is how awesome it is in the big picture…*"Somewhere over the rainbow!"* At an altitude of 35,000 feet, Heaven didn't even seem so far away. The song, *"How great Thou Art,"* was silently resounding in my thoughts as if I was on a mountain top and my voice was echoing across the Grand Canyon, but I was the only one who heard the music.

Someone said, "I pray every day, but I have never asked God for anything personally. He is busy with important things." I said, "Don't you know how big God is? Do you think when He is helping me find a parking place on a snowy day, He is neglecting some life threatening situation in Iraq or Afghanistan? The greatness of God is beyond our wildest imagination or ability to comprehend.

He is Alpha and Omega, the beginning and the end. He is the first and the last. Before anything existed, He was there!!! God, in His foreverness, created everything that exists out of nothingness. He simply said, "Let there be," and there was! We live in a time/space world. God occupies eternity! Eternity exists outside of time. He doesn't only see the past and the present. He already knows the future. God knows every event that will transpire all over the world. He sees the " big picture."

We open the puzzle box and dump the puzzle pieces on the table. Without the picture on the front of the box, we wouldn't have a clue about the image that will appear when it is completed. As the puzzle pieces are fit together, the picture begins to emerge.

As the right pieces form the big picture in life, we can see the bright side. Instead of seeing today is partly cloudy, we see it is partly sunny. Instead of seeing the cup as half empty, we see it as half full. Instead of seeing only the worst of times, we look for the best of times. Instead of only looking for the bad in people, we look for the good. Instead of looking at what we have lost, we see what we have left. We see the blessings in each new day and the beauty in each new season. We hear the sound of music that lifts the soul. We see beyond our sorrows and reach for joy.

If you are still looking at the black clouds in the rear view mirror, it is possible to miss seeing the rainbow. Look for God's promises. Look for ways to bring answers to the problems in your world. Look for hurts to heal and needs to meet. Look for ways to give hope to the hopeless. Look for the Divine appointments in the big picture.

A resident in our Assisted Living Center spent months putting together a two thousand piece puzzle. When the puzzle was finished, one piece was missing. The empty space revealed the shape of the Cross. She said, "I only see the missing cross." The cross became the big picture. Our lives can never be complete without the Cross. On my Holy Land tour, we visited Golgotha, the place of the skull, where Jesus hung on the cross. At the foot of the hill was a garbage dump. I was heart broken. My husband said, "It is a vivid picture of what happens when we kneel at the Cross. We leave the garbage of our lives and receive His love and forgiveness."

The cross is connected to purpose and destiny. Real joy is found in fulfilling the purpose for which we were created. We each have a cross to bear. When we take up our cross to follow Jesus Christ, we see behind the scenes by faith and trust Him with the big picture. Romans 1:17 says, "The just shall live by faith."

The picture will not be complete until we step from time into eternity. There are famous cities in the world that I never expect to see. But one day Gail Gammill will walk through the gates of that Holy City and my eyes will see its unprecedented splendor. Sometimes, I have been disappointed when visiting far away places that were not as magnificent as I expected. Alongside the beauty of the man-made structures, there was trash in the streets and signs of decay.

Jesus said, "Let not your heart be troubled; you believe in God, believe also in Me. In My Father's house are many mansions; If it were not so, I would have told you. I go to prepare a place for you." He promised, "I will come again and receive you unto Myself; that where I am, there you may be also," John 14:1-3,6. All roads do not lead to Heaven. In verse six, Jesus claims indisputably, *"I am the way, the truth, and the life. No man comes to the Father except through Me."*

The final book of the Bible, The Revelation, gives us a glimpse of the "Big Picture." Darkness has no substance. It's merely the absence of light. "For now we see in a mirror, dimly, but then face to face," 1 Corinthians 13:12. In Heaven there is no need for the sun or the moon because of the radiance of the glory of God. There is no night. There isn't daily newscasts reporting the rebellion, crime, moral decay, and the pain of tragedies that are happening in the impoverished cities in our world. In Heaven there will be no sin, no sorrow, no hunger, no pain, no sickness, nor dying. God, Himself will wipe every tear from our eyes. Can you imagine living in a world with no hospitals, no mental institutions, no cemeteries, or prisons? Come with me on a tour of Heaven...

Each of the twelve gates in the Holy City, the new Jerusalem, are made of solid pearl. The foundation is adorned like a glistening, prismatic jewel box with the twinkling iridescence of twelve precious gemstones. The dazzling, variegated color in such a magnificent, exquisite exhibit is unimaginable. The brilliance in the sparkle of the combination of jasper, sapphire, sardonyx, sardius, chalcedony, emerald, chrysolite, jacinth, topaz, chrysoprase, beryl, and amethyst is viewed as commonplace as the sand on the sea shore.

The streets are pure gold, like transparent glass. The walls are made of a sparkling diamond-like Jasper. The intensity of the radiant incandescence of the manifested presence of God produces a rainbow of chromatic color, beyond even the most spectacular fireworks displays. On either side of the boulevard is the tree of life, each continually bearing twelve fruits. The flowers bloom with the freshness of countless springtimes. A pure river, as clear as crystal flows from the throne of God, and we shall behold Him in all of His Glory!!!

One Sunday evening two couples walked into our storefront church in Birmingham, Alabama. They each made a decision to commit their lives to Jesus Christ. One of the men was a commercial building contractor. While helping plan for the construction of our new church, he developed lung cancer. He had smoked since he was only twelve years old. He surrendered his life into God's hands to fulfill His purpose and destiny. He miraculously had no pain and no fear. He witnessed to every care giver who entered into his room about the greatness of God. He actually won more people to Christ in six months than many people win in a lifetime.

In the moments just before his death, you could hear him singing in the corridors of the hospital, *"I saw the light. No more sorrow. No more night."* He looked up and asked, "Can you see the light?" His description of the radiant splendor of Heaven gave us a visual picture of the Holy City.

As he was leaving this world, I will never forget his words. He said, "Jesus is here. Tell everyone, this is the finest peace and contentment." Wow! What an incredible illustration of perfect peace. I began singing, *"What a treasure I have in this wonderful peace, buried deep in the heart of my soul. So secure that no power can mine it away while the years of eternity roll."* Peace comes instantly when we place our trust in God. Trust Him with your why's in the big picture!

Disease cannot change your eternal purpose and destiny. God is sovereign. He had just healed and literally re-created the kidneys of a woman in our church who was in the final stages of cancer. Her medical doctors were shocked and documented the miracle. It was amazing! We expected God to heal Orie also. Herschel asked God, "How do I explain this to my congregation?" God spoke to him, "I healed him for all eternity." My trust is not in my faith. My faith is in my God.

I heard about a man who took his small child into an elevator. The child was standing beside him as it filled with people. From the child's point of view she was surrounded with legs and feet. When she panicked and started screaming, her father picked her up and held her in his arms. Instantly, she began laughing. Her circumstances hadn't changed. The elevator was still crowded with people. She was still in a tight place. The only difference was that now she could see the same situation through her father's eyes.

Another puzzle piece in the big picture is found in 1 Thessalonians 4:16-17, "For the Lord Himself will descend from heaven with a shout, with the voice of an archangel, and with the trumpet of God. And the dead in Christ will rise first. Then we who are alive and remain shall be caught up together with them in the clouds to meet the Lord in the air. And we shall always be with the Lord."

Our Heavenly Father desires to lift us up into a place where we can see our circumstances and future through His eyes. It is a place of trust. Our questions will fade into oblivion. One day, we will see the whole picture that surpasses the ability of the greatest artists of all time to portray. It is beyond the description of every author's ability to articulate. The dynamic orchestrated sounds and rhapsody in the musical performances of the most famous composers will not compare with the ecstasy produced in Heaven.

Today we can only imagine, but the day is coming when we shall behold its beauty. In God's Book, "The End" is "The Beginning." How exciting that God, Himself, planned "your" place in the big forever picture! He knows where you are.

CHAPTER THIRTY TWO
THE LILY OF THE VALLEY

Wouldn't it be great if life had only mountain top experiences! When our children were teenagers, we took them on a family vacation to Pikes Peak in Colorado. It was an exhilarating feeling making it to the top of the mountain. The perspective from that view is so different. There are no surprises. You can see for miles. Everything looks so small and insignificant in comparison to those up-close insurmountable obstacles we don't see coming in our daily lives.

God never promised that every day would be perfect. He only promised He will be there. I love and often quote this Scripture: "Fear not, for I have redeemed you; I have called you by your name: You are Mine. *When* you pass through the waters, I will be with you; And through the rivers, they shall not overflow you." He said, "*When* you walk through the fire, you shall not be burned, Nor shall the flame scorch you. *For I am the Lord your God,*" Isaiah 43:1-3. I can hear my Heavenly Father saying, "Don't be afraid. You're not alone."

Did you notice that He used the word, "when," not "if"? I had no idea "when" I woke up one morning that this was the day my dad would go to heaven. Every crisis experience we face in life is another opportunity to trust God. In the best of times, He holds my hand. In what seemed like the worst of times, God held me.

My family believed God could do anything and I witnessed miracles like they were ordinary events. Dad almost died several times throughout my life. As a small child I remember being so scared when he became ill. The doctor made house calls back then. One day, I heard him say, "He won't live through the night." Dad laid there motionless. His eyes were open, but it was obvious he didn't see us in the room. The only sound was him gasping for breath and a strange rattle in his chest.

People from the church came and gathered around the bed praying. I ran outside and knelt behind the bushes in the alley. It was my secret place where I talked to God. I have no idea how long I was there. When I returned to the house, my dad was sitting on the side of the bed eating soup, and everyone was praising God for the miracle.

One day, Dad walked down the aisle to the altar at church and announced, "It's time. I'm ready to go to heaven." Three days later, he ended up in the hospital and I received the call that he was dying.

Within thirty minutes my daughter and I had our bags packed in the car and were on our way to Kansas. When we stopped at a pay phone to check in, my husband informed us that dad was already in heaven. He prayed with us, advised us to get some rest, and continue our trip the next morning. Every motel we passed had a 'No Vacancy' sign, so we drove all night.

We were on a dark highway, but God's GPS knew our exact location. I closed my eyes and silently began quoting the Twenty-Third Psalm. "The Lord is my shepherd, I shall not want." When I got to the part, "Yea, though I walk through the *valley* of the shadow of death, I will fear no evil; for You are with me. Your rod and Your staff they *comfort* me;" an amazing thing happened. The fragrance of the lily of the valley entered the automobile. Deana immediately asked, "Mom, do you smell that?" The sweet, distinct aroma stayed in our car all the way to Kansas.

The essence of Jesus Christ, who is referred to as *'The Lily of the Valley'* invaded the atmosphere letting us know He was there. Deana turned on the radio. The words of a song were painting an incredible description of the Celestial City. With tears rolling down our cheeks, we began singing songs about Heaven. As we focused on what my father was experiencing in that Holy City, God's peace filled our heart. We knew... "All is well."

We had an unexplainable awareness that we were being escorted by Jesus Christ, *'The King of Kings,'* and the angelic hosts all the way home. The next day was Father's Day. I was sad that I wouldn't get to spend the day with my father. I wondered why dad couldn't have waited one more day. Suddenly, I understood. He wanted to be with his dad on Father's Day. God answered his prayer.

When I returned home there was a gift waiting for me in the mail. It was a beautiful pin with a lily of the valley silk floral arrangement. The card had a picture of lilies of the valley. A few years later, I laid the little pin on my mothers dress at her home-going celebration. I didn't have to tell either of my parents, "Goodbye." I just said, "I will see you later."

In Matthew 6:28-34, Jesus reminds us that just as our Heavenly Father takes care of the lilies of the field, He will take care of us. If you are walking through a valley experience, meet the "Lily of the Valley" in the twenty-third Psalm. This message will gently remind you that He is there. He knows where you are.

CHAPTER THIRTY THREE
THE TORNADO

I grew up in Kansas. We had an underground tornado shelter in our back yard. During tornado season, my dad kept it supplied with water, food, and flash lights. There were three different sounds on the alarm system in my home town. One signal was only a warning that weather conditions could possibly produce a tornado. Another siren meant a tornado has been sited. Take cover immediately! The third sound announced the storm was over. Afterwards, Dad would take us with him to assess the damage. Once, a whole small town was blown away. The memory is still indelibly stamped on my mind. As a child, the threat was very real. I witnessed the destruction firsthand.

Our church Youth Camp was the highlight of my summer. Prior to camp, on payday mom gave us the money for our camp fee. I kept a bag packed and took it to the storm cellar with me, in case the house was blown away. When the storm clouds started forming on the horizon, we joined hands and prayed. I wasn't afraid. I knew God was there and He would be there when the storm was over.

When we lived in Cleveland, Tennessee, the news channel began flashing the warning that we were in the path of a tornado. I took the children to the lower level of the house. When the storm passed over, the damage near us was catastrophic. One house exploded into pieces like a mountain of rubbish. The house next door to it was untouched, and the garbage can was sitting in the driveway.

Another house was completely blown away as if it never existed. The front page headlines of the local newspaper had a picture of a couch sitting on the foundation. The family had no time to take cover. They joined hands and prayed. It was amazing! The house and everything in it was gone, except the sofa on which they were sitting. Their house could be rebuilt. Their family was spared!!! God, Himself, was their shelter in the storm.

On one occasion a tornado was happening while the children were at school. The students were all sitting under their desks. The teacher said that our little girl was exclaiming in her southern accent, "Don't worry!!! God's-a saving us!" Through the years, anytime we were in a situation that was out of our control, someone in our family repeated her words, "Don't worry! God's-a saving us." There are all kinds of storms in life. There is no way to predict the fierce winds of adversity. There is not an advance warning, but God is always there to bring peace in the midst of the storm.

My sister, Donna, and her husband, Charles, were pastors of a church in Ramona, Oklahoma. They were en-route home from a Youth Rally, when a teenage boy under the influence of alcohol left his side of the road. The first car swerved, missing the impact, but the teenagers in the middle car were hit head-on. Charles and Donna were in the car behind them. One minute Diana, their sixteen year old daughter was laughing and waving to them in her rear view window. The next minute she was gone. The driver, along with four other teenagers were killed when his car spun out of control. It was devastating.

We arrived the night before the funeral. The air was so filled with grief, you could cut it with a knife. It felt like the oxygen was evacuated from the room. My husband began praying, "God, let your peace fill this place." I can't explain it, but the Holy presence of Jesus Christ, *'The Prince of Peace,'* instantly charged the atmosphere with a serenity that was supernatural. As the family worshipped, it sounded like we had been joined by angels.

A funeral for the four teenagers was held in the high school auditorium. Family members, along with many teen-age friends, made a decision to commit their lives to Jesus Christ. God can bring good out of every situation. The tragedy in that little community will always be remembered by those whose lives were forever changed.

At times life seems out of control like a raging tornado that is destroying everything in its path. The fear of anything that is life threatening can make it feel like your world is coming to an end. In Matthew, chapter fourteen, the disciples were in another ferocious storm in the middle of the Sea of Galilee. Their boat was being tossed by the waves from the fury of the wind. They were terrified.

When Jesus came walking on the water, one man asked permission to come to Him. Jesus answered, "Come." Peter stepped out of the boat on faith and actually walked on the water. Every time we walk in obedience to God's Word, it is the same principle. By faith, we can walk on top of our troubles. It wasn't until Peter looked down at the waves that he started sinking. Jesus was there to rescue him. Keep your eyes on Jesus.

When the winds are raging and the earth is like sinking sand, He will be the Rock beneath your feet. He is your shelter from the wind and the rain. Jesus Christ is the peace in the eye of the storm. The presence of God is an invisible force that is felt from the core of our being. Hebrews 11:1 says, "Now faith is the substance of things hoped for, the evidence of things not seen." Doubt and fear vanish in His presence. Say it out loud with me, "Lord, I believe." He knows where you are.

CHAPTER THIRTY FOUR
THE WEDDING

When my son was a little guy, he was in awe of Wonder Woman. He told me, "When I grow up, I'm going to marry her." He did!!! ...Seriously, she is a blond rendition of "Wonder Woman." While attending Oral Roberts University, he met Nan, the amazing girl of his dreams.

On the day Nan was going to a banquet to accept a full scholarship to the Kansas State University, she received a call from the Admissions Director at ORU. The night before, she had seen Nan's name on a computer screen in a dream. She searched her computer and discovered she was the winner of the prestigious Blue Chip Academic Scholarship Award. Nan knew her dad would never give his consent. The director said, "I know God has other plans." She asked God to change her dad's mind. It happened! That miracle changed her destiny.

At her first Concert Choir class, Dana was seated in the next row. In their final semester, Dana came home on Christmas break and returned to school with an engagement ring in his pocket. One day he made an announcement, "She said, Yes!" Nan had been planning her wedding since she was ten years old. She had already chosen the color of her bridesmaid's dresses, so I went shopping.

The wedding wouldn't happen until July, but I found the perfect dress at an after Christmas Sale. When I hung the dress in my closet, a strange thing happened. It was just a passing thought, "You won't wear this to the wedding. You will wear it to your funeral." That's bizarre! I put it out of my mind and completely forgot it happened. Three weeks later, I began having pain in my left leg. After an examination, the doctor concluded that it was possibly a sprained muscle and would take a few weeks to heal. The pain continued to increase and it became impossible for me to bend my knee. Further testing revealed a tumor and the doctor scheduled the surgery and the possibility of other post medical treatments.

When I walked outside, a question out of nowhere entered my mind, "Would you be willing to die for me?" It sounded spiritual. I remembered the words about the dress in the closet. I wondered, "God, were you trying to prepare me for this?" For one split second, I almost answered, yes, but realized this is not the voice of God. He sent His Son to die in our place, so that we can live! If I had accepted the lie, I don't believe I would still be here today.

The Bible declares in Proverbs 18:21, "Death and life are in the power of the tongue." I confronted fear. When I heard reports of people who died with similar symptoms, I refused to be afraid. I declared, "I will live and fulfill my purpose."

Both, my son and my sister, Donna, called with this promise: "I shall not die but live, And declare the works of the Lord," Psalm 118:17. The next day, the director of Flame Fellowship left this message for me; "I'm not sure what this means to you, but God told me to tell you, you will live and not die, and you're going to a wedding."

The week before the surgery a prayer group from church came to my house to pray for me. It felt like someone touched my leg. I opened my eyes, but no one was near me. Heat, like a supernatural power surge, remained in my leg for several hours making any post surgery treatments unnecessary.

The surgeon successfully removed the tumor, but he had to cut through each muscle in my thigh. My leg was dead weight. I couldn't move it. My brain stopped sending automatic signals to those muscles. Even after it had healed, I would catch myself still dragging that leg. I had to purposely remember to tell my knee to bend before each step. I went through several months of physical therapy and literally had to learn to walk all over again, but thank God, the tumor was benign.

I stayed on a bed in the family room until I was finally able to walk upstairs. I remember watching a terrible storm outside my French doors. The wind was so fierce, it blew the deck away. No one was there but me and God. I wasn't afraid. I had a promise from God, "I would live and not die." God would take care of the storm also. By the way, I went to the wedding and walked down the aisle. I believe in the power of God. It isn't possible to convince me that miracles can't happen because miracles have happened to me all my life.

On another occasion, after a routine mammogram I was informed that I needed to see a surgeon. I watched the technicians conducting the test as they located the tumor on the screen. Suddenly, I heard one of them say these words, "It looks like it is shrinking." They watched the tumor disappear before their eyes. It was an amazing experience! They continued repeating the procedure, but were unable to find it anywhere. The tumor was gone!!! It no longer existed. The doctor could only explain that the surgery wouldn't be necessary. What an incredible miracle!

Perhaps, someone reading this book just received an alarming report from the doctor. I just want to encourage and remind you that prayer changes things!!! A need is a miracle in disguise. Miracles happen when you believe! God has a promise for "you." He knows where you are.

CHAPTER THIRTY FIVE
THE ELEPHANT EARRING

My husband and I were traveling on a mission tour to China. En-route, we made a stop in Seoul, South Korea. The Ministry of Dr. David Yonggi Cho on Prayer Mountain with 100,000 members was a life changing experience. The atmosphere was literally charged with the presence of God. When we left for Hong Kong, it was like colliding with the powers of darkness. We had to refuel in Taiwan. The stop turned into a mini crash landing. No one was hurt, but we had to change planes.

When we were on our way for the second time, the plane began making a high pitched screeching sound and began making a descent. I asked the flight attendant if we had turned around. She said, "No." Since there was nothing under us but water, I attempted to disengage the emergency floating apparatus under my seat. Herschel asked, "What are you doing?" I reminded him that I don't know how to swim. Very calmly, he assured me, "You won't need it."

I interpreted that to mean we're going to heaven. I began praying for God to comfort everyone back home when they heard the news. The plane began shaking like it was going into convulsions. The overhead luggage doors flew open and luggage was flying out. The flight attendant said in her Korean accent, "Lean your head back and try not to scream." The only other sound was the quiet prayers of sixty-seven ministers on board that flight. I was surprised that I wasn't afraid to die. Suddenly, it was over and the plane was back on its course.

When we landed in Hong Kong, the passengers applauded with cheers of relief. My husband asked an airport official what happened and was told it was pilot error. The 747 was going too fast through the jet stream and he lost control of the plane. The screeching sound was the result of the plane in distress. They said that it should have been impossible to reverse the lethal situation. I said, "I may have to learn to speak Chinese." Even the thought of getting back on a plane made me feel nauseated.

That night, I realized that one of my hand-carved elephant earrings was missing. My son had given them to me when he returned from an overseas trip. I mentioned it to someone in the hotel lobby. The next morning, a lady who had overheard the conversation walked up to me. She was holding the elephant earring. She had just happened to pick it up somewhere out on the street. I couldn't believe it. I had been on boats. I had walked in places where people were living in cardboard boxes. I could not have possibly retraced my steps. Wow! If God could prearrange for my little lost earring to be returned, He certainly would arrange for me a safe return home. When it was time to leave China, I was on the plane!

At times, I still had reservations before getting on a plane. After boarding in Canada for an overseas flight, we were informed the flight was delayed because of mechanical problems. I was scared. I told our flight attendant about my horrific flight to Hong Kong. She assured me the plane wouldn't take off unless it was repaired. I prayed, went to sleep, and woke up as we landed in London.

The return flight home had the same pilot, same flight attendant, and another delay because of problems with the aircraft. Finally, we were in the air. The flight attendant said the pilot wanted me to join him in the cockpit. It was a big 747. He said, "Flying is one of the safest ways to travel. Ships float because there are designed to float. Planes fly because they are designed to fly." He explained how the law of lift overrules the law of gravity. He didn't want me to be afraid to fly because of a bad experience. To be invited into the cockpit was unbelievable. I was impressed!

The next time I got on a plane, I was going to California. While waiting in Chicago to board my connecting flight, I overheard two guys talking, "It's like someone is going before us, preparing the way." I asked, "What's going on?" They said, "You certainly won't have to worry about this plane being hijacked. Federal agents are on board. You couldn't be more safe." They boarded first as if they were body guards of a passenger.

While waiting for take off, a pilot and his entire crew boarded the passenger part of the plane. The pilot was seated right in front of me. I asked him what was happening. He traded seats with the person beside me. Because of some delays this trip would exceed the time that they were officially allowed to fly. He informed me that he personally flew the plane here, but another crew was sent for this part of the flight. He explained every aspect of our flight before it happened.

A famous television minister was sitting across the aisle from me. I thought, "This is crazy." There are two federal agents, two pilots, two airline crews, a preacher, and who knows how many angels on board. I'm going to California! I knew I never had to be afraid to fly again. God was the One who was going before us, preparing the way. We don't have to be fearful. Fear visits us but we don't have to let it stay. Our faith in God produces courage. Courage causes fear to disappear.

Years later, I lost the elephant earring again. I had been visiting patients on almost every floor of the hospital. I asked God to show me where to look. I had a mental picture of a leaf, so I started walking toward the parking lot. It was springtime.

There were no leaves on the ground, but to my surprise, a leaf was lying beside my car. Under it was my elephant earring. God's GPS had to have sent His angels to arrange its location, because anything that concerns me, concerns Him. I wish you could know how much He cares.

I was sitting in church this past Sunday behind a young mother. Throughout the entire service she was picking up each of her newborn twin babies the moment they made the least whimper. I had twenty dollars in my purse. God told me to give it to her and tell her, "God loves you."

After the service I walked over to greet a lady I hadn't seen in a couple of years. She handed me two twenty dollar bills and said, "God told me to give these to you." I thought, "Really, God? With all the billions of people in the world, is there anything you miss? How do You do this?" He not only knows where we are, He is actively involved in our life. He is always watching over all of us. I have to say it one more time: "God loves *you*. He knows where you are."

"Trust in the Lord
with all your heart;
And lean not on your own
understanding;
In all your ways acknowledge Him,
and He shall direct your paths."
-Proverbs 3:5

CHAPTER THIRTY SIX
THE LOST AND FOUND DEPARTMENT

I am sure God has a lost and found department. What is it about the Gammill family that someone is always losing something? I don't think there is anything more frustrating than trying to find something that has been lost or misplaced. You know... the insanity of repeatedly going back to the same place and looking one more time, or trying to retrace your steps in your mind. Where did I go today? How long has it been gone? When was the last time I recall seeing it before realizing it was missing?

And then, out of nowhere something miraculous happens and it shows up, or you suddenly have a newsflash and know exactly where it is located. I am convinced that we have a guardian angel who is sent on GPS assignments to help us retrieve all of our lost items. If I had a quarter for every time a family member has lost their keys or misplaced an important item I would leave them a note saying, "Gone shopping!"

One evening, my daughter-in-law was frantically looking for something. She was distraught when she finally admitted she had lost her wedding and engagement rings. Dana encouraged her to go to bed and they would look tomorrow.

After she was asleep, Dana asked God where she lost them. He woke up at 3:00 a.m. and knew exactly where to look. He drove across town to the dry cleaners and felt impressed to stop the car. The second he opened the door, he looked down and saw them sparkling on the pavement. How they had been protected from all the busy parking lot traffic was amazing. I call that a miracle!

He returned with the rings and asked Nan, "Did you go to the dry cleaners yesterday?" Instantly, she recalled sitting in the car putting on hand lotion and had left the rings in her lap. They had inadvertently dropped to the ground when she got out of the car. Anything that is important to you, is important to God.

My grandson, Michael, lost his high school class ring he had designed with symbols that were important to him. He was the president of his Senior Class. Surrounding a red stone, on one side it has his name with a Bible and a cross. The other side says, President, and has a gavel and a lamp. It had been missing for eighteen months. While on a family vacation in Florida, they went to a little

Cuban restaurant. They were waiting to be seated, when out of nowhere, they saw something drop from the ceiling. It landed and bounced on the floor in the middle of where they were standing. It was Michael's class ring! It was one of those crazy, unforgettable, unexplainable, how did this happen moments. We are still in awe when it comes up in conversations. It is beyond amazing!

One time, Dana and Nan were watching a movie. He had just cashed his two week salary check for three hundred dollars and slipped the envelope into his inside coat pocket. When the movie was over, he discovered it was missing. The theater personnel helped search between the seats where they were sitting. It wasn't there.

Dana prayed and believed it would be found and returned to him. Several days later, he received a call that the cash was mysteriously discovered in the exact spot they had searched. Every dollar was still there. It was a miraculous answer to prayer.

One morning, Dana left the house in a hurry and forgot something. When he returned to his car for the second time, he accidentally locked the keys in the house. When he checked to see if any other doors were unlocked, he found his keys hanging in the lock on the back door. It was amazing! He had gone in and came out the front door! He had not been in the back of the house. Things like this have nothing to do with luck or coincidence. God is the head of the the lost and found department. When you ask for His help, angels are already on the way! There is no other logical explanation.

When Dana moved back home from Oral Roberts University, as we were unloading the trunk, we realized only one of his ostrich skin cowboy boots made the trip. His dad had brought them back from Korea and they were his favorite shoes. He searched all of his bags and boxes and completely emptied out the car. No boot! Instead of throwing the remaining boot away, he put it in his closet.

Weeks later, he opened the trunk and the cowboy boot was lying there. He thought someone was playing a joke. When he looked in the closet, the other boot was still there. How do you explain something like that? He wears a size eleven. It was too big to slip through a crack. It is too late to tell me angels are not real or convince me that God doesn't care about every detail of our lives. He has intervened too many times.

Deana was employed by a television network. The week of Christmas, she cashed her salary check and was planning to go shopping. After work, she discovered the money was missing. They searched the entire studio, but it was nowhere to be found. We asked God for a miracle. On Christmas Eve, it showed up in plain sight at the TV station.

Whether it was hand delivered by an angel, or the person who took it felt remorse and brought it back, God answered our prayer. On Christmas morning, Deana had presents for everyone. While God is taking care of our family, He is watching over every family on the planet. Our Heavenly Father is concerned about everything from the smallest detail to the colossal issues we face in life.

Have you ever been lost? It is an uncomfortable feeling when that unfamiliar sign appears. You realize you took a wrong turn, and now you are traveling in the wrong direction. Finally, you see an exit so you can find your way back to the right road leading to your destination.

But what about those times when wrong choices are taking you down a path that is leading you away from your Divine purpose? It is not too late. You can change the course of your destiny. God knows! He is orchestrating answers to your prayer even before you ask.

On this journey through life we can experience loss much greater than missing items. Jesus told a parable about a son who lost his way, and a father who lost his son. The young man asked for his inheritance and wasted it all on riotous living. One day, the money and his friends were gone. He found himself living in a filthy pig pen, eating with the swine. Jesus said, "He came to himself."

The son regretfully said, "I will say, Father, I have sinned against heaven and before you. I am no longer worthy to be called your son. Make me like one of your hired servants." His father welcomed him with open arms. He gave him his best robe. He put sandals on his feet, a ring on his finger, and celebrated his return. He said, "My son was lost and is found," Luke 15:11-32.

This story is a picture of our Father God. His grace pardons and covers a multitude of sins. One of the most beloved songs in America is, *"Amazing grace, how sweet the sound that saved a wretch like me. I once was lost, but now I'm found. I was blind, but now I see."* If God is concerned with the little incidental things that are missing in our lives, how much more does He care about us?

God sent us a personal invitation. Jesus said in Revelation 3:20-21, "Behold I stand at the door and knock. If anyone hears My voice and opens the door, I will come in to him and dine with him, and he with Me. To him who overcomes I will grant to sit with Me on My throne, as I also overcame and sat down with My Father on His throne." Is your Heavenly Father waiting for you to RSVP? His GPS will guide you. God always knows where you are.

CHAPTER THIRTY SEVEN
THE SEED

My parents and childhood pastor taught me the seed and harvest principle. In our little backyard garden I learned that you will reap what you sow. Apple seeds can only produce apple trees. If you plant a watermelon seed, in a few weeks you will be eating a watermelon. It was always fascinating watching the tomatoes appear on the vines and the little plants in each row produce exactly what was planted. It works on every level.

The Bible explains this in Hosea 8:7, "They sow the wind, And reap the whirlwind. The stalk has no bud; It shall never produce meal." Job 4:8 says, "...I have seen, those who plow iniquity and sow trouble, reap the same." It works in the negative and the positive. If you sow harshness, you will reap hostility. If you sow kindness, you will reap kindness. If you sow mercy, you will reap mercy. When you forgive, you will be forgiven. What you give, you will receive.

As a child, I learned that one penny out of every dime belongs to God. My parents gave each of us an allowance of ten cents every week. God only required one penny. All of the remaining pennies were mine. I discovered when you give a tenth of your income to God, He multiplies the rest. Do you know what you could do with nine pennies in a candy store? My friends asked me if I would put their pennies in the candy and gum-ball machine, because I was always getting one of the speckled balls that could be exchanged for a nickel. Why? Jesus answered that question when He said in Luke 6:38, "Give and it shall be given to you..." I have seen this principle demonstrated all my life.

Tithing is a test. It proves to God what and who, has first place in your heart. In Mark, 10:17-22, the story is told about a man who came to Jesus and asked the question, "What shall I do that I may inherit eternal life?" Jesus replied, "Sell whatever you have and give to the poor, and you will have treasure in heaven." The man sadly walked away. It was only a test. He failed it... Jesus said, "For where your treasure is, there your heart will be also," Matthew 6:21.

Tithing gives God an opportunity to prove His covenant with you. "Honor the Lord with your possessions, And with the first fruits of all your increase, So your barns will be filled with plenty," Proverbs 3:9-10. Tithing literally stretches your dollars. When you do your part, God is faithful to do His part.

The Scripture in Malachi 3:8-10 explains both the blessing and the curse that follows obedience or disobedience. To not tithe is putting your money in pockets with holes in them. You will only reap what you sow. You can't reap a harvest from a seed that was never planted. Someone asked, "Should I tithe on the gross or the net of my income?" Herschel responded, "Only tithe on the income which you want to be blessed." Creative purchasing and blessing begins with giving to God what belongs to God.

Invite God to go shopping with you. Our Father God loves to provide for us. Years ago, I was shopping for an outfit for a Western Night family event at the church. I saw the perfect skirt with bright colors and braided trim. It was on sale for twenty five dollars. I decided to wait and went to Value City instead. As soon as I walked into the store, I saw the exact same skirt with a vest to match hanging on a sale rack. It was only ten dollars. I laughed when I saw the bargain! It is a scriptural principle. He gives us our desires when we trust His judgement for what is best for us.

I was at the mall one day and noticed a necklace that exactly matched a pair of my earrings. It was Victorian with a porcelain pink rose and pearls. I admired it. It wasn't expensive, but I didn't need it. I never mentioned it to anyone. The next night I went to church and a lady walked up to me with a gift. Inside the box was the necklace. She said, "I was shopping today. This necklace reminded me of you." God doesn't give me everything I want. Sometimes, He just wants to remind me He was there. When you give God first place, He is at the top of your list. And guess what! You have always been at the top of His list!

I was given fifty dollars one time for my birthday. I spent it on a gorgeous white skirt trimmed in lace. There was a beautiful blouse that exactly matched with the same label. Same price! It would be perfect for my next wedding anniversary. I hoped it would go on sale. That night after church, a guest approached me. She said, "I watch you and your husband on your TV show. God told me to bring this to you. Go shopping!" It was a fifty dollar bill. I had more compliments on that dress than any I have ever worn. I always said, "Thank you, God gave it to me."

I bought an arbor for my garden at a ridiculous price. I had checked on it so many times to see if the price was reduced, that the clerk put my name on it as soon as it went on sale. I was shocked when I saw the tag: Price $300/now $35." Jesus stated in Matthew 7:11, "If you then, being evil, know how to give good gifts to your children, how much more will your Father who is in heaven give good things to those who ask Him!" The love of our Heavenly Father amazes me.

Shopping for my daughter's wedding dress was exciting. She knew exactly what she wanted. She had seen the dress in the window of a bridal shop weeks before. I asked the clerk if it would go on sale. She replied, "Absolutely not!" I gave her my phone number and told her to call me when it goes on sale. Two days later, my phone rang. The dress had been discontinued. The only one in the store was her size. We bought it for a fraction of the original price.

Does God always do that for me? No. If it is gone, either I didn't need it, or He has something better. I am not attached to temporal things. Material things lose their luster when compared to that which is eternal, which leads me to my next point. Keep things in perspective. Things can contribute to happiness, but happy feelings are temporary. Compulsive buyers who shop for the purpose of filling a void will never have enough. Those who understand the secret of giving will always have more than enough. The more you give, the more God will stretch what you have left.

One Sunday, I had a one dollar bill and a ten dollar bill. I felt that God wanted me to give my best gift in the offering. Immediately, I gave the ten dollars. On Monday, a little girl placed a ten dollar bill in my hand at the grocery store. As I was leaving the store her mother said, "God said to give you ten more."

I asked God to show me what to do with the twenty dollars. The next day, a lady who was a guest at church on Sunday met me at a cafe for breakfast. Both of her parents were deceased. She had no siblings or children and was feeling very alone. I asked God for guidance. I told her, "You will never be alone. God wants you to know He is here. In fact, He is paying for our meal."

I realized the money in my purse wasn't mine. When I told her the story she had tears in her eyes. God used my gift to remind her that He loves her. I gave ten dollars in the offering and ended up with twenty more dollars to give. Not only was I privileged to bless my church, but I became a part of helping God bless someone else.

When Dana and Nan were expecting their first child, they felt impressed to give away all their savings. Even though they didn't have insurance coverage for the hospital expense, they decided to trust God and give it anyway. Their insurance had expired because they had changed companies. An amazing thing happened! They were given favor and informed that the entire bill was paid in full.

A minister declared to them that God was going to provide all of their expenses after the baby's birth, including diapers for one year. One afternoon, as Dana was driving away on the church parking lot, he reminded God of the promise. He was out of diapers. A delivery truck drove up beside him on the church property. The truck was filled with diapers of every size. When he unloaded them, not only were there enough diapers for a year, but there were enough to stock the church nursery. Really? A truckload of diaper donations? Here is this word again, "Amazing!"

Recently, our grandson, Michael, felt impressed to give a substantial offering to a ministry in Ireland. It was a sacrificial step of faith because He and his wife were having mechanical problems with both of their cars. He was told the repair on his car would cost more than it was worth. He was faced with the financial strain of having to buy another vehicle. He took it to the Hyundai dealership to see if it was possible to trade the car in a purchase agreement. They kept it to assess the damage and would get back with him.

When Michael received the call to pick up the car, it was repaired. He was shocked. The problem turned out to be a factory recall. The manufacturer paid the total cost. You can't out-give God! In the meantime, Michael was given another car. Since his Santa Fe was repaired, he had an extra car to give to someone else in need of transportation. His offering became the gift that kept on giving. I have discovered, "What you make happen for others, God will make happen for you."

Someone said, "Who plants a seed beneath the sod and waits to see believes in God." When you plant a seed, you expect it to produce whatever you planted. Every harvest begins with a seed.

Inside of everyone of us, God planted a seed of faith. My husband said, "Your employer sets your salary, but you and God establish your income." Herschel habitually gave something away every day. A missionary, who gave His life for the sake of the Gospel said, "He is no fool who gives what he cannot keep, to gain what he cannot lose."

In eternity it will no longer matter how much you accumulated on earth. The questions that matter are: What seeds did you sow? What do you have to give? The more you give, the more God will place in your hand, so you can give again. If you eat your last seed, it will become your last harvest. Never spend your last dollar. Give it away!

I could share a lifetime of stories about creative purchasing. The greatest one of all is found in John 3:16, "For God so loved the world, He gave His only Son." Jesus paid the ultimate price for our sin. Congratulations! He did it for *you*! When you receive Him as your personal Savior, you get the best bargain of all time; you exchange death for eternal life; you exchange your sorrow for joy; despair for hope; weakness for strength ... In Him is everything you need. He knows where you are!

CHAPTER THIRTY EIGHT
THE QUESTIONS

As a child, I accepted anything anyone said at face value. I rarely asked questions. My little sister wondered about everything. "Where does water come from?" I said, "The water faucet." She asked, "But how does it get there?" I said, "Who cares?" So she grew up and became a school teacher and I'm still deciding what I will be when I grow up!

I was privileged to have two wonderful children. I could say, "No, no," to my son. He would put his little hands behind his back and never touch the forbidden object. The same scenario only seemed to increase my daughter's curiosity to discover why. She needed to know "why" before she even knew how to talk. They learned and processed information differently.

I discovered that there are two ways to learn. We can learn by listening or by experience. We can either learn from our mistakes or from observing the mistakes others, which takes me back to the beginning again. Even the first man and woman struggled with making these choices.

Have you wondered why God created us? God created humanity in His own image because He wanted relationship. The Bible records that God placed the first man and woman, Adam and Eve, in the beautiful Garden of Eden. In the cool of the day He walked with them. There was only one tree that God told them not to touch. Eve was tempted to understand why. The tempter told her if she ate of the tree of good and evil she would be as wise as God. She took the fruit and ate it, and then, convinced Adam to do the same.

That one decision changed everything. When they heard the sound of God walking in the garden, they hid because they were afraid. God asked, "Adam, where are you?" They had chosen to go their own way. Because of disobedience they were sent out of the garden. While many people in this twenty-first-century ask "Where is God," He is still asking today, *"Where are you?"* God asks the question so we will think about our answer. Sin separated us from God, but never from His love.

Did you ever wonder what God was doing before He created us? He said, "Before I formed you in the womb I knew you," Jeremiah 1:5. "Your eyes saw my unformed substance, and in Your book all the days of my life were written before ever they took shape," Psalm 139:16 Amp. God knew us first, He knows us best, and He loves us most! He loved us before the foundation of the world.

At my old home I had a beautiful garden with flowers of every color. It was fun watching to see which perennial would arrive next. Nestled beside the flowers was a stone engraved with the word, "Believe," and an altar that had been built by my husband's grandfather. I loved to kneel there and talk to God. Many times, when my grandchildren came to visit, they went to the garden and talked to their Heavenly Father before they came into the house. Through prayer, we can have instant access and personal communication with the Almighty supreme highest level of authority... the Creator of the universe! That is more than amazing!

How about going to the garden with me? I am reminded of a familiar song written two centuries ago. The elderly people at The Inn often ask me to sing it to them. If you know the tune, sing it out loud with me. *"I come to the garden alone, while the dew is still on the roses; And the voice I hear falling on my ear, the Son of God discloses. And He walks with me, and He talks with me. And He tells I am His own; And the joy we share as we tarry there; None other has ever known."*

Obviously, the writer knew God personally. He wrote, *"He speaks, and the sound of His voice is so sweet, the birds hush their singing. And the melody that He gave to me, within my heart is ringing..."* Have you talked to God today? Is God waiting for you? Do you know Him?

God already had a plan for redemption when sin entered into the first garden. If only one person could have lived a sinless life, it would have set the criteria for all. But everyone has sinned and missed the mark. His own Son was willing to pay the penalty.

At some point in life, every person faces the big question. Before the crucifixion, Pilate, who was the governor asked, "What then shall I do with Jesus, who is called Christ?" The crowds creamed, "Crucify Him!" Jesus could have called legions of angels to the rescue. Instead, He went to the Cross willingly. Jesus understood His mission to bring reconciliation between God and humanity.

Jesus was born to die so that we can live and experience eternal life. We can choose to accept or reject Him. Two thieves were hanging on each side of Christ on the cross. One rejected Him, but the other recognized Him as the Messiah. Jesus said, "This day you will be with Me in paradise."

We each come to the crossroad of decision. The question is: *"What will you do with Jesus?"* I was only four years old when I invited Him to come into my heart. He has been been there in the good times and the bad times. He gives life purpose and makes it worth living. Christianity is not about a religion. It is about a relationship! It is a Divine spiritual connection.

In the Old Testament, a man named Job asked the age-old question that has plagued the human race universally for centuries: "If a man dies, shall he live again?" *Is there life after death?* Even nature itself answers that question. If God gave even the little rose bush, whose blossoms wither and die before winter, the promise of blooming again in springtime... there is no way you and I, whom He created in His own image, will ever cease to exist. The question is not "when" but, "where?"

I was on an elevator that was so crowded, it was invading our privacy perimeter. It kept stopping on every floor and made a loud, disturbing noise. In that, too-close-for-comfort, awkward moment, I commented, "It sounds like the elevator is doing aerobics." A man and woman started to get on and got right back off. A little boy said, "Hi...bye. We'll see you in another world." I said, "That depends on where they are going."

People who don't know why they are here wander aimlessly through life. The truth is that you were born with a purpose. Life is not about time. It is about eternity. The most important question you will ever answer is: *"Where will you spend eternity?"* When civil laws are broken in our country, there are consequences depending on the severity of the crime. "The wages of sin is death, but the gift of God is eternal life through Jesus Christ our Lord," Romans 6:23. Choose life. Choose Christ!

You may not know the answers to all of your "Why's," but you can know the One who holds your life in His hands. You may not know what your future holds, but you can know Who holds your future.

In the Old Testament, God introduced Himself as being "the God of Abraham, Issac, and Jacob." Someone asked my youngest grandson when he was only three years old, "What is your name?" He answered, "I'm Blake, from God." That was a profound declaration! How awesome that Blake understood. "He is the God of Blake." Every one of us can place our name in that statement. When we understand *where* we came from, we can trust God with *where* we are going.

Ask God the hard questions and trust Him with the answers. In Isaiah 41:10, God, Himself said, "Fear not for I am with you." He assured us, "Be not dismayed, for I am *your* God. I will strengthen you, Yes I will help you. I will uphold you in My righteous right hand." The answers to the difficult questions about the meaning of life will lead you to God. He knows where you are.

CHAPTER THIRTY NINE
THE ANSWERS

During my growing up years, I spent a lot of time in my room. I never felt alone. I was always aware of God's presence. I talked to God about anything and everything... the details of my day, the things I didn't understand, my feelings when I was sad or upset, excited or glad. He was always there. He became my best friend. He answered my prayers. I learned that there has never been a problem for which God doesn't have a solution. I rarely have taken "no" for an answer about anything without looking for a way to change that conclusion; but I also learned that sometimes "no" is an answer.

I read about a little girl who asked God to change her brown eyes to blue. The next morning she ran to the mirror and was heartbroken that God didn't answer her prayer. She exclaimed, "You said God always answers our prayers!" Her mother asked, "Isn't no an answer?"

When she grew up, she became a missionary. Her assignment was in a remote village where women were afraid of foreigners. She couldn't speak into their lives because they would run away. Since the women had dark skin and brown eyes, she made up a coffee mixture and rubbed it into her skin to change its pigment. She changed her appearance to look like them and was immediately accepted. Carrie remembered her childhood prayer. "No" was the right answer! It wouldn't have happened without her brown eyes.

Yesterday, I found a beautiful writing pen in the back of a drawer in my dresser. I have never seen one like it. The top of it is filled with crystals. I wondered why I stopped using it just because it ran out of ink. When I went to Office Max to pick up a new refill, the clerk couldn't figure out how to take it apart. We took it to an older gentleman who came to the same conclusion and said, "There is no way to replace it even if we had a cartridge this size." I couldn't imagine there not being a way to resolve this issue.

On the way out of the store I decided to try one more time. I showed it to the clerk at the checkout counter. She twisted the opposite end of the pen and it immediately began sliding apart. I took it back to the same young girl and she excitedly found the perfect size refill. She couldn't believe I didn't give up. I replied, "Most of the time, where there's a will, there's a way." She smiled and said, "Wow! I learned something new today!" It takes perseverance to achieve success.

I try to learn something new every day, but how many times do we forget to take our own advice? I didn't throw the pen away when it quit working. I just admired it in the box. How many times do we do that in life? How many times do we give up looking for answers and just accept a situation at face value? How many times do we forget lessons we learned in life and find ourselves going around the same mountain, repeating the same mistakes? How many times do we rely on our own expertise or searching for remedies without first asking God for help?

This week we had a family dinner at our Assisted Living Center. The theme for the event was, "The Roaring Twenties." It was a classy affair with a big band concert. The table centerpiece arrangements were wine bottles filled with beads and feathers. Afterwards, during the clean-up time our activity director put her index finger into a wine bottle to remove the decorations. Unfortunately, her finger got stuck and started swelling.

She was surrounded with solutions. Everyone was surfing the Internet on their cell phones asking for answers. The bottle was placed in hot water and ice was placed on her hand. The kitchen crew tried to lubricate her finger with olive oil. The director of maintenance brought a hammer and was sure he could break the bottle and solve the problem. The nurse told her to go to the emergency room before it cut off circulation. Finally, my son, the pastor arrived, walked over, gently pulled and it slid right off. When asked how he made it happen, he replied, "I prayed."

Sometimes we don't get answers because we aren't asking the right questions. We ask "why" but we are not ready for the answer. When my grandson, Michael, was two years old, he had to ride in his car seat for eighteen hours from Ohio en-route to Florida. Explaining to him that he was going to Disney World would not have changed his level of frustration. Mickey Mouse meant nothing to him because he had no frame of reference. Sometimes, we have to wait for the answer.

There are some times in life when no one has the answer. When the doctor doesn't have a cure and Wall Street is having a bad day are not reasons to give up in despair. Perhaps someone reading this is going through a traumatic circumstance that is beyond your own ability to resolve. When you are facing a crisis and the aspirin bottle is not going to fix it, go to the source you can trust. Almost every day I pray the Prayer of Serenity: "God, grant me the serenity to accept the things I cannot change, to change the things I can, and the wisdom to know the difference." Knowledge lacking wisdom and understanding is meaningless. The problems we face cause us to seek for answers.

Sometimes, answers come in unexpected ways. In a book store, I noticed a beautiful wall hanging that was elegantly framed and lying on a discount table. It was the "Serenity Prayer." The frame was damaged. I looked at it but walked away. Before leaving the store, I decided to make the "as is" purchase anyway. Walking to my car, I realized how easy it was when I made a decision to accept what I couldn't change.

It is all about the decision. I chose to receive the message and accept the flaw on the frame. I gave it to my granddaughter. She was disappointed for not being chosen in a singing group at school. Allison didn't give up. The next year she tried again and was the first one chosen. She accepted the temporary existing situation but changed the final outcome.

Dana was on a flight returning from a mission trip to Mexico when he had a mental picture of a plane in a terrible storm. He prayed for a safe trip. When they arrived in Houston for their connecting flight there was a ferocious storm. He told his friend beside him, "It will be okay. I've already prayed about this." Within five minutes after clearance to leave, the plane was in so much distress luggage was flying out of the overhead compartments. His friend asked, "Do you think you should pray again?" Dana asked God to make a way through the storm. Suddenly the pilot said, "If you look out your window, a strange thing has happened. The storm separated leaving a path in between for the plane to enter." With volatile dark clouds and lightning on both sides, there was total calm as they passed through the atmosphere. It was an incredible portrayal of the extraordinary answers God has waiting for us in life.

Scientific research is seeking answers for incurable diseases. Politicians are seeking answers for the never ending problems in every arena of life. Government officials are seeking answers to stop the crime and violence in our cities. World leaders are seeking for peace in a world that is being threatened by terrorism. We can give up in defeat or trust God for answers. God will either help us change our situation or give us the inner strength to pass the test. God placed determination in each of us. The secret is found in "not giving up."

I don't have all the answers, but I know the One who does. Look to God for the solutions. He is the source of all wisdom. The answers we don't get in this lifetime will be revealed in the life to come. He has already written the last chapter. When the last page of our history book is recorded, God will still be there. He has and will *always* have the correct "Final Answer." He knows where you are.

CHAPTER FORTY
THE OVERCOMER

"Overcomer!" Shout it out loud! Even the sound of the word generates energy. When a speaker asks the question, "How many of you want to be an overcomer?"... without debate, every hand will up in response. No one wants to be defeated, but which would you like to hear first... the good news or the bad news? The bad news is that to become an overcomer, there must be something to overcome. Do you still want to be an overcomer?

For those of you who would raise your hand, I have good news for you. Two thousand years ago, as if Jesus were listening to our morning news channel, He sent a text message telling us to cheer up: "These things I have spoken to you, that in Me you may have peace. In the world you will have tribulation; but be of good cheer, I have overcome the world," John 16:33.

Jesus Christ was preparing his disciples for some inevitable persecution, suffering, and even failures they would face. His promise in that passage gives a strategy and assurance that it is going to be okay.

The first part of the promise is dependent on the second part. He promises peace and then explains how to attain the promise.

Let's look at the verse again. "These things I have spoken to you that in *Me*, you may have peace." Jesus said that our peace would be found in *Him*. Where? ..."*In the world.*" When? ..."*In times of tribulation.*" He is saying to cheer up because you can have peace in the midst of it all. He addressed the answer to the question, "Why?" when He said, "I have overcome the world." The peace that Jesus gives is founded on *His triumph*.

The word "victorious" is the description of what it means to overcome. Jesus conquered defeat and tribulation on the cross. He won the victory over sin for every person who would ever live on planet Earth. Every one of us would need a Savior. We would all need mercy and forgiveness. He conquered death, hell, and the grave when He died in our place and rose again.

The word "tribulation" involves those difficulties ranging from disappointments to tragedies. The struggles we face in life can take us to the edge of despair in search of a way out. The overcomer discovers victorious living in the faith that God knows where I am and is in control of my life. "God is our refuge and strength, A very present help in trouble," Psalm 46:1.

To be of good cheer means: "To have courage." Peace is the special gift we receive when we take courage and place our complete trust in God. Jesus remembered us in His will. He said, "Peace I *leave* with you. My peace I give to you; not as the world gives do I give to you. Let not your heart be troubled, neither let it be afraid," John 14:27.

When we handle problems in our own strength, we reach for the peace the world gives. It can end up with all kinds of drama like panic attacks, confusion, remorse, fear, and hopelessness. The outcome of whether we overcome the dilemma is not determined by the trauma that happened, but depends entirely upon how we react or respond to the conflict. Tribulations are merely temporary interruptions in the cycle of life. They are only a test. We have a choice. We can sink into despair or accept the challenge and make a decision, "With God's help, I am an overcomer!"

Every day you face opportunities to be victorious. Unexpected challenges present the privilege to prove that God's grace is sufficient. This lesson can change your thinking. Stop speaking negative words about yourself. Take the "t" out of can't. Make positive declarations every time you look in the mirror: "Something good is going to happen to me today! I am a winner! I refuse to be defeated!" "My help comes from the Lord, Who made heaven and earth," Psalm 121:2.

This past week I felt as if I was living in a bubble and nothing seemed real. Literally, hundreds of people came to give respect and honor to a man who had always seemed bigger than life. We stood for seven hours as people kept streaming through the line with sincere love and support for our family. After spending fifty five years of marriage and ministry together, my husband stepped into eternity. He is no longer a part of my present, but he is still in my future.

Our family is facing the reality that we have to experience the grief of his absence. The overcomer realizes that life is a continual process of new challenges. It begins with a decision. I will not surrender in defeat! I choose to deal with grief by counting my blessings. I will add up my joys, not my sorrows. In moments when tears become like a waterfall or the winds of sorrow are taking my breath away, the peace of God arrives.

Sometimes unresolved issues or pain from the past revisits us. It is a part of the healing process. Daily walking in love and forgiveness heals the hurts of yesterday. Facing every day with faith seals the hopes for all of our tomorrows. My husband always said, "God didn't call us to run from life. He called us to take hold of life." You can overcome every obstacle course. The worst of times come unexpectedly, but we get to make our own best of times. With God, triumph will prevail!

I can almost hear someone asking, "But how do you overcome difficult situations when life isn't fair?" How do you get over those somebody-did-me-wrong-songs that leave you in pain you can't bear? The answer is forgiveness. Forgiveness is a choice. Jesus modeled forgiveness on the cross when He prayed, "Father, forgive them." Holding on to hostility, anger, resentment, bitterness, and hatred creates a wound that cannot heal until the infection is removed. These three words, "I forgive you" is the password to turn it loose and let it go.

The day of our daughter's twenty fourth birthday, I bought her a bouquet of helium-filled balloons. I told her, "Each balloon represents someone who deeply hurt you. Go outside and release them." I watched the tears roll down her cheeks as she declared the words, "I forgive you," and let them go one by one. One balloon burst and fell. She buried it in the back yard. She had been stalked and violently attacked. It was devastating. As she released the balloons, she "let go" of the offense, and turned her worst of times into triumph. Over time, I watched as she smiled through her tears, ministering healing and deliverance to the broken hearts and broken dreams in the lives of others.

This past week, my daughter shared a personal testimony. She had just lost her father who had stood with her through the trauma of the whole ordeal. He modeled the image of her Heavenly

Father's everlasting love, as he had held her and cried with her. One day she received a phone call. The man who assaulted her asked for forgiveness. Deana told her dad she was able to say, "I forgive you." Herschel said, "I can't do it." His heart was still broken.

Sunday morning was Valentine's Day. On the way to church, he said, "I can't go to the pulpit if I can't live what I preach." He asked Deana to sing before the message. She shared how God helped her to extend forgiveness. People started coming to the altar. One woman had carried un-forgiveness for years toward a drunk driver who had tragically killed her son in an automobile accident. She wept and released forgiveness.

Herschel stood before his congregation and said, "I need to be the first one at the altar." His actions modeled more about forgiveness than he could have taught in a hundred sermons. The memories he leaves behind are still teaching us.

Many years later, Deana was pastoring a church in Indiana. Several women were murdered and their bodies were found in a corn field she passed going home every day. Some of the victims were last seen at Walmart. She began being stalked again. She was terrified. Everywhere she went, the same man showed up watching her from a distance. Fear gripped her. She started having nightmares.

One day, the man followed her into Walmart. She made a decision to face her enemy. She turned around, walked right up to him and spoke to the demons, "I know you! I have met you before and I command you through the name and the blood of Jesus to get out of this region!" He started backing up and backed right out of the store. She never saw him again and the violence stopped!

Through Christ we absolutely have the ability to cope with anything that comes our way. The Bible declares that nothing can separate us from God's love... "Yet in all these things we are *more than conquerors* through Him who loves us. For I am persuaded that neither death nor life, nor angels nor principalities, nor powers, nor things present nor things to come, nor height nor depth, nor any other created thing, shall be able to separate us from the love of God which is in Jesus Christ our Lord," Romans 8:37-39.

..."For whatever is born of God overcomes the world. And this is the victory that has overcome the world—our faith," 1 John 5:4. My husband used to say, "There is something down inside of me that will live as long as God lives. I will never run out of living." We read these profound words engraved on an old tombstone: "Death, thou has conquered me. I, by thy dart am slain. But Christ has conquered thee and I shall rise again." I am more than a conqueror because God says I am!

I don't know what you are facing today, but I know that when you invite Jesus Christ into your life, you are linked to a winner. Through Jesus Christ *you* are an overcomer! Jesus said in Mark 9:24, "If you can believe, all things are possible to him who believes." Say this with me: "I believe!!!" He knows where you are.

CHAPTER FORTY ONE
THE STRESS FACTOR

The word, "stress" is not foreign to anyone on the planet. It may sound different in every language, but the meaning is the same. We all experience stress on some level every day of our lives. It is a major factor to deal with because stress that is not managed can produce major, serious health issues. Medical statistics state that seventy to ninety three percent of all disease is related to stress.

In high stress situations, I find myself standing at attention in a perpetual, intense, rigid posture. I have to take a deep breath and force my body to relax. Constant worry, fear, anxiety, anger, pain or inordinate grief raises our stress level. Eventually, it can weaken the immune system.

Stress happens! For some, it could happen while they are walking down the aisles of the grocery store knowing the balance in their checkbook; for others, it may be driving in heavy traffic on a big super highway rushing to get to work on time. Whatever the cause, we can deal with it or suffer the consequences that occur.

Stress doesn't go away overnight because it is so daily. Overcoming it is a process. Someone asked me at church last night, "How are you?" I said, "I'm okay." I walked over to welcome a visitor. When I introduced myself he asked, "Oh, are you the widow of the minister who just died?" I stayed so cool, calm, and collected I could have won the Best Actress Award, but my head was spinning. That word had never been mentioned. The word "widow" triggered a rush of emotions.

My daughter was the evening speaker. She said, "Today is the day the Lord has made. I will rejoice and be glad in it! Rejoice today! It is an act of the will. I *will* rejoice! We want our circumstances to change, but our circumstances are waiting for us to change. The Hebrew translation of the word "rejoice" in Psalm 118:24 is attached to worship."

I began to focus on God's presence. The center of my being goes beyond my feelings level... It is connected with my Creator; it is united with Christ; it is where I draw my peace, my strength, and my joy. I found this incredible secret in Psalm 16:11: "You will show me the path of life. In Your presence is fullness of joy; At Your right hand are pleasures forevermore."

We can enter into His presence in our pajamas the first thing in the morning. We can meet with Him on the pages of His written Word. We can have an audience with Him in the classroom, on the job, in our prayer closet, on the front line of a war zone, or in the intensive care at the hospital -whenever and wherever we are. That is beyond amazing! God is not "I Was." He's the Great "*I Am!*" He was here yesterday. He is here today... and has already walked in all of our tomorrows.

David said in Psalm 18:6, "In my *distress* I called upon the Lord..." The chapter describes stress and reveals when and why the Psalm was written. The circumstances that David is referring to happened during the time he was hiding from cave to cave. David had killed Goliath, the Philistine giant, who had been terrorizing all of Israel. When he became the favorite in the palace, King Saul was filled with jealousy and attempted to take His life.

David penned these words three thousand years ago and we are still repeating them. The rest of the chapter tells how God delivered him. *"Distress"* is a strong word. One of the meanings is: narrow and constricted, a place with no way out. Distress is a claustrophobic feeling of not enough space, too much pressure, trouble on top of trouble. In the book of Psalms, over and over distress shows up, and right beside it is God declaring Himself to be the God who delivers us. Whether it is little things that turned into big things or feeling like the world is coming to an end because something catastrophic happened... stress finds us!

The day that the church caught on fire left our grandson Michael and his fiancé with the dilemma of finding another location for their wedding. The 'Hold the Date' announcement had been mailed months before and the invitations were already printed waiting to be sent out the next week. They were expecting eight hundred people to attend their service and the revised invitations had to be in the mail in seven days.

It is difficult to find a place available to hold that many people on short notice. The stress started mounting. Jacee stopped to pick up her wedding dress the week of the wedding and was informed that someone failed to complete the alterations, and now it was too late. Sometimes, it's that one more thing you have to add to your list that sends you over the edge. I'm sure there were tears, but Jacee kept smiling.

That evening, they were sitting in a conference next to the guest speaker. He leaned over and told Jacee, "Everything is going to be okay, even to the seams of the wedding dress." The minister didn't know about the problem, but God did! No other bridal shop could fix the dress since it wasn't purchased in their shop. A woman overheard the conversation. She was formerly employed to sew wedding gown alterations and offered to tailor the dress." There is no problem too big for God ..."We walk by faith and not by sight," 2 Corinthians 5:7.

On their wedding day, we were sitting downtown in President McKinley's former church. It felt like a royal wedding. The building is magnificent. It is a historic, very regal architectural structure with incredibly beautiful stained glass windows. It was a majestic moment listening to the wedding march as the bride came down the aisle. Stress dissipated instantly in the excitement of the vows that were being made between two people to share the rest of their lives together.

When it feels like you are in a cave with only one entrance and a train is heading toward you full speed ahead, it is time to do as David when he said, "In my distress, I called upon the Lord." God gives us instant coping power. Psalm 18:32 says, "It is God who arms me with strength, and makes my way perfect. He makes my feet like the feet of deer; And sets me on my high places,"

God didn't deliver David "from" the situation. He delivered him right "in" the midst of it. People are always looking for ways to escape their problems through synthetic solutions that disappear into a fantasy world that doesn't exist. Sadly, they wake up with the same difficulties still staring them in the face.

While David was hiding in a dark cave knowing in only a matter of time he would be discovered, he wrote the famous Twenty-Third Psalm: "The

Lord is my shepherd, I shall not want... Yea though I walk through the valley of the shadow of death, I will fear no evil for You are with me." He didn't say, the Lord is "*a*" Shepherd. He referred to Him as "*my*" Shepherd... my Light, my Sword, my Shield, my Rock, my Refuge, my Fortress. It was David's relationship with God that carried him to the pathway of living by faith.

It is ironic that when Saul received word to return to Jerusalem, David was only a stone's throw away. Wow! Did you see what just happened? God is faithful. In Psalm 18:6, David spoke of his distress, but added, "He heard my voice from His temple, And my cry came before Him, even to His ears." Instead of reacting in despair, he made a decision to respond with faith. 1 Samuel 30:5-6 states that David was greatly distressed, but he encouraged himself in the Lord.

Sometimes, we have to encourage ourselves. I can hear the cheerleaders of my past saying, "When you get to the end of your rope, tie a knot and hang on." That knot is faith in God. I can hear my mom saying, "God's got it all under control." I can hear my dad, who was a Golden Glove boxer saying, "Keep that Mefford chin up." You don't need a mountain with a cave in which to hide. I can hear Pastor Dave Lombardi saying, "All you need is faith in God." Deana gave me a plaque that says, "Worry ends, where faith begins."

James 1:2 says, "Count it all joy when you fall into various trials." Wow! It sounds like he was saying, "Welcome stress!" Now that's an assignment! You and I get to experience some opposition today. I can't wait. Really? Wilbur Wright said, "No bird soars in a calm." The law of lift requires some opposition to get the plane off the ground. The stress in life combined with prayer and faith in God can get us airborne.

The law of lift overrules the law of gravity. You can rise above your problems. You can see beyond the trouble. God can make it a blessing in disguise to thrust you into your destiny. Rejoice! Trust Him. He knows where you are.

This is our Blessed Assurance:

"The Lord is my shepherd;
I shall not want.
He makes me to lie down in green pastures.
He leads me beside the still waters.
"He restores my soul..."
-The Twenty Third Psalm 1-3

CHAPTER FORTY TWO
THE RESTORATION PROCESS

When I woke up this morning, these three words "The Restoration Process" invaded my thoughts. I knew they would take me on a journey. The word "restore" is associated with these words: renew, recover, repair, or return to a former condition. Restoration takes us *"Back to the future."* It sounds like a fantasy science fiction movie.

Sometimes, life can feel like a drama in the movie theater. It keeps recycling. Haven't I been there, done that? Believe me, after seventy five years, life becomes a re-run. However, making it through the experience once gives me the assurance that I can do it again. It is exciting to start over when you know that, "In the beginning, it is God... At the ending, it is God... And it is God on all the pages of our life in between." The past, the present, and the future all join hands with God in the center of it all. The faithfulness and the greatness of God is mind-boggling. It takes me to a place beyond my greatest ability to imagine.

I remember the year 2000. It always seemed so far away, but at midnight on December thirty-first, 1999, the calendar flipped over and it was January, one. We didn't only move into a new year, we changed centuries. We began our journey into a whole new millennium.

There is no pause button on the clock. While we are sleeping, the sand is slipping through the hour glass. The hands on the clock continue to move second by second... minute by minute... hour by hour... day by day. The months swiftly pass and another year, another decade, another century, and another millennium has gone by. Time marches on. In a few hours, today will be gone, and the time spent will be recorded.

Have you ever wondered what it would be like to go back in time? Suppose you could actually step into a time capsule and be transported into a time and place you have only read about in a history book. Wouldn't that be an adventure!

I had the privilege of visiting a place called, "Tara" in Clark, Pennsylvania. It was a replica of the scene in which the movie "Gone With the Wind" was filmed. Upon arrival, we were greeted by ladies in long gowns like those worn in the 1800s. We viewed a video describing what life was like in that era, including clips of the Civil War. Each generation has its own struggles and victories.

We have the advantage of learning from those who have lived before us. Sometimes, we think life in the 21st Century is more stressful than that of former generations. But can you imagine life without all of the information we have in this high tech society? For example, Columbus didn't know the world was round. It was only a theory. It took a lot of courage to sail into the sunset not knowing if he would fall off when he reached the other side of the world.

...Or what about the pioneers who set out in covered wagons to carve out a future in the Wild, Wild West? The world isn't actually so different. It is still dangerous. Because of nuclear capabilities, there is a constant threat of war, worldwide chaos, destruction, and the fear of total annihilation from the planet.

The Bible declares that when man is in one accord, one mind, and one language, he can accomplish anything he can imagine. My mother traveled on a covered wagon from Missouri to New Mexico. I remember when interplanetary travel was just a figment of the imagination. Today, a rocket ship can travel 2500 miles per hour through outer space for a distance of 230,000 miles to the moon. Past communication systems went from messages that were delivered by horseback, to the Morse Code being sent over telegraph wires and radio waves. Today, we hear and see instant verbal and visual messages transmitted by satellite from the other side of the globe in seconds. Someone said, "The imagination of the mind is a mirror of the future."

Unfortunately, the mind is a tool for both good and evil. Have you longed for a second chance? Have you ever wished you could go back, erase a mistake and start over? It is impossible to go back and relive even one minute of your life. But I have good news for you. I know a way to go back to the future. There was a moment in time when the Creator, Himself, joined hands with humanity. It was a place where the past would connect with the present in order to change the future for all eternity through the birth, life, death and the resurrection of the Messiah... the promised Savior of the world.

Come with me on a journey that will carry us back in time to thousands of years ago. You won't need a suitcase. Ladies, you can even leave your make-up case behind. You won't even have to purchase a ticket. The price was paid in advance. We won't stay long. Fasten your seat belt. All chairs and lap trays should be locked in their upright position. Please remain seated for the duration of the trip. Secure for take-off. We will be cruising at a level of ten million feet... faster than the speed of sound or light. We will be going back in time arriving at our destination in approximately... five seconds. Prepare for landing.

Ladies and gentlemen, we have just arrived at that moment when God first drew out His plan of the ages... The earth is without form and an empty waste. Darkness is covering the face of the deep. Nothing exists but God. Isaiah 45:18 Amp. says, "For thus says the Lord Who created the heavens, God, Himself, Who formed the earth and made it, Who established it and did not make it to be a worthless waste; He formed it to be inhabited. I am the Lord and there is no one else."

Get ready! Watch this! The Spirit of God is moving over the face of the water. The voice of God is thundering the words, "Let there be light!" God is bringing order out of chaos. God literally spoke the universe into existence. If He can restore the earth in only six days, He can restore and bring order out of the chaos of the troubled times in our lives. Let hope arise!

Picture in your imagination God scooping up the dust and forming the first man in His own image. He gave him the ability to love and enjoy all that He had created... But Adam became deceived and violated his privileges. The consequences of his disobedience was separation from God. Spiritual darkness invaded the earth, but God already had a plan for redemption. Please check to see that your seatbelt is fastened. Prepare for take off... Watch for the star. God's spotlight will be presenting the arrival of Jesus Christ, *'The Light of the world.'*

Prepare for landing. An innocent teenage virgin has just miraculously given birth to a baby boy. On a silent, holy night in a crude animal shelter outside a village called Bethlehem, the story of the first Christmas is unfolding. The characters who are gathering around the stall holding the infant include the virgin mother, a carpenter, and some shepherds who had witnessed through a host of angels, the announcement of the birth of the Lord Jesus Christ. The promised Messiah... the Son of God has arrived on planet Earth!

Wise Men riding on camels are following the star. They are on a mission. This event will change the history of every generation to come. Jesus Christ left the splendor of Heaven. He came and became like one of us to bring restoration and redemption for all humanity Fasten your seat belt. All systems clear. Prepare for take off.

...Please remain in your seats. Flight attendants prepare for landing. This is where we go back to the future. We are here by invitation. Jesus Christ was born to die so that we can live. He took our place. At the foot of the old rugged cross, every man, woman, boy, and girl through the eons of time has been invited to leave their sins and receive peace and forgiveness. Every one of us are invited to accept Jesus as our Savior and Lord. The moment you believe, you will change your future for all eternity! Leave your regrets and failures at the cross. All systems clear. Fasten your seat belts and prepare for take off...

One day, we will make our last approach to our final destination. We only have 365 days a year. Imagine making the most of every one of them. Every day you enter a moment in time and space you have never traveled before. Each day ushers in changes and new opportunities for growth. So celebrate today! It is your gift from God. Refuse to fear the future or worry about yesterday.

Welcome to Trinity Eternity Airways, flight #777. All seats and food trays will be left in their locked and upright position. You won't have to take your belongings with you. On that day, you will hear the words, "We will be arriving at the Gates of Pearl shortly. Prepare for landing!!!" Soon you will hear the echo of His voice resounding from the corridors of Heaven, "Welcome home. Enter into the joy of your Lord."

Restoration is the process of transformation that makes all things new. What do you need from God? Do you need Him to restore your joy or peace today? Do you need forgiveness, correction, or deliverance in some area of your life? Take hold of God's promises and prepare for the future.... He knows where you are.

"Celebrate Life
and it will celebrate you!"
You can find something to celebrate
every day.

"A celebration captures a moment and
makes a memory that lasts a lifetime."
-Dana Gammill

CHAPTER FORTY THREE
THE CELEBRATION OF LIFE

Celebrations in life keep my imagination working overtime. I look for something to celebrate every day. On my seventieth birthday my grandson, Michael, showed up with a limo and a sunflower. It's true... "If you celebrate life, it will celebrate you." This morning, I remembered that because of all the whirlwind of personal family disasters, we missed spring and summer this year. The chill of winter is already in the air. Oh well, that means Thanksgiving and Christmas are just around the corner and they are my favorite holidays. I am so excited!!! I am project oriented, so my mind is already doing cartwheels.

Every chapter in our life has something we can celebrate. Life is filled with opportunities to give recognition and honor to those we love. A party provides an invitation to bring people together to make memories that last for a lifetime. Most of our celebrations end up around the table. I love when the kitchen becomes our family room.

Some of our most important family celebrations and special events are traditions that we inherited from a former generation. Celebrations are great ways to preserve the moment. My son said in his book, *Keys for Successful Living,* "This moment in time will only happen once, so make your once upon a time worth happening."

At our Thanksgiving meal when the children were growing up, everyone had the choice of wearing a construction paper pilgrim hat and collar or an Indian headband. We talked about how the first Thanksgiving became an annual national holiday for giving thanks to God. Everyone gets to express something for which they are thankful. When we understand the importance of thanks-living, every day becomes Thanksgiving.

It is our custom to pray before each meal. I place Scripture cards at the place settings and we each read our promise. On all special occasions, we receive Communion. Each of us take a piece of bread and dip it into the goblet of grape juice in remembrance of Christ's suffering for our sin. At dinner celebrations, we eat buffet style and set the dining room table with themed centerpieces. My best china and crystal are used for any occasion. My family are the most important people in my life. I am always looking for new opportunities to communicate to all those I love, "You are special."

Birthdays are huge for the Gammill family. The meal of the person being honored is always served on our special, "It's your day" plate. I always ask God what gift He would have me give, which often becomes a significant personal theme for the coming year. Once, I gave Dana a rainbow by putting a prism in the window to remind him of God's promises. The sunlight produced rainbows like sun-catchers all over the room. Birthday cake, candles, balloons, and streamers are always part of the event. The parties and gifts are all planned to communicate the message, "You are a gift from God. Today is your day!"

On Christmas Eve, our church has a candlelight family Communion Service. Each family gathers around the table where a gift-wrapped box is lifted off the Communion Sacraments. It reminds us that our greatest gift is not found under our Christmas tree, but on the tree that became a cross where God "gave" His only Son.

We enjoy "Nanny's" chicken and noodles recipe, Christmas cookies, and take a drive to see the Christmas lights. Christmas Day is packed with eating festive favorite foods, football, opening presents, the Christmas story, and blowing out the candles on our Jesus' birthday cake. Dana presents everyone with a single, red rose. At midnight on New Year's Eve, we pray over the new year, make a toast decreeing blessings, and have a party.

After my dad went to Heaven, my mother came to visit. Since we lived a thousand miles apart, we decided to celebrate everything we had missed in a lifetime. Every day was a surprise. It was a warm summer day, but we decorated all of our Christmas trees and celebrated Christmas for a day. The next night we had a traditional New Year's Eve party. We ate black-eyed peas, pork and sour kraut, and shared New Year's resolutions.

For Valentine's Day we made valentine cards and heart-shaped cookies. Everyone got chocolates. On our St. Patrick's Day we discovered you can make anything green with food coloring, even eggs. I played the accordion and we sang Irish songs.

Since our highlight of Easter is the special music and pageantry at church depicting the crucifixion and resurrection of Christ, the children produced their own drama. We had an Easter Buffet and an Easter egg hunt. Decorating the eggs is a family affair. Our July 4th celebration was a barbecue in the backyard. Everyone got sparklers and flags to salute. We crowned Mom "Queen For A Day." We even celebrated Ground Hog Day and played hide and seek with the grandchildren.

On Grandmothers Day, we brought her flowers. When Mom fell and broke her wrist, we had a Pity Party. We gave her lace handkerchiefs, signed her cast, passed out tissues, and on the count of three exclaimed, "No more tears!" My mom called the family back home and said, "All they do is go to church and have parties." There is something to celebrate every day if you look for it. Just put a candle in the meatloaf and celebrate life.

Celebrate the season. ...So you hate winter! Get over it! Watch a winter video produced in a ski resort. Sit inside where it is warm, drink some hot chocolate and watch the skiers sail down the slope. ...So it's raining! Wear sunglasses, anyway. Sometimes, you have to make your own sunshine.

One year I defied the Ohio weather and surprised my family with Christmas Dinner in Hawaii. We greeted each other at the door with "Aloha" and Hawaiian leis. I had ornaments on the palm tree in the living room. The meal was served in luau style with music from the Islands... Another year, I had a Santa Fe' Christmas. I found a big cowboy Santa to put on the table with a string of red hot peppers and bright red lights. The menu included all of our favorite Mexican food. Michael, our grandson showed up wearing a Santa suit with a cowboy hat and cowboy boots.

This year, I'm having a Story Book Christmas with a Nutcracker cartoon video so Isabella can dance with all the ballerinas. Storybook characters are under the tree with a train racing around the track and a Charlie Brown nativity set. The highlight is the greatest story of all, "The First Christmas." Isabella carried a battery operated votive candle. We sang every verse of *"This little light of mine. I'm gonna let it shine!"* I love it when we turn out the lights and sing my favorite carol, *"Silent Night."*

One year, I took my family on a trip around the world. We brought places from far away into our home. Every week, I prepared a meal with recipes from a different country. We visited the library to learn about their customs and located them on the map. The festive music with its distinct sounds created a feeling of being there. The table center pieces were souvenirs from various trips. We learned a few words in each language. We ate Chinese food with chopsticks, seated on the floor around the coffee table. Papa wore a sombrero at our Mexican dinner. We celebrated life in other countries and we never left the house.

One Memorial Day, I asked everybody to bring something that represented a favorite memory. Both of my children brought a trophy I awarded them for being the Best Son and Best Daughter when they were teenagers. I brought my mother's Bible. Allison brought the ivory satin dress her mother made for her baby dedication. Michael brought something from a favorite family vacation and Blake brought a football. I asked my husband what he brought. He forgot. He said, "I brought myself." It is one of my best memories.

We have choices every day of our life. When life is difficult, it is easy to miss the moment. One time I had prepared a special meal with candlelight and a bouquet of fresh flowers on the table. Herschel didn't come home for dinner. Afterwards, en-route to the church, I decided whatever his excuse is I'm going to be mad anyway. Instantly, I repented. I rolled my car window down and told my bad attitude to get out. When I arrived, my husband was praying with a woman who was distraught. Her daughter had just been kidnapped. I couldn't imagine what she was going through.

My little girl always brought me color papers from school. One day I asked her, "What did you make me today?" She said, "I made you happy. I came home." Don't take life for granted. Bake some cookies. Prepare after school surprises and have a Welcome Home party every day.

I look for ways to turn tears into smiles. It was a dark, gloomy day and my grandchildren were crying because everyone in the family called saying they couldn't make it for dinner. I said, "Well, they are going to miss having dinner in a cave, in the rain forest." I threw a blanket over the kitchen table. I put the sounds of the rainforest on a music tape in the stereo and opened the kitchen window to let the rain inside. We ate our meal in the cave under the table and the room was filled with laughter.

You can scatter some sea shells on the deck, put a kiddie pool in the yard, and with a few squirt guns or water hose pretend you are on the beach. Don't wait for a perfect day. A little imagination can roll the clouds away even on a rainy day. If you can't afford a vacation, go camping in a tent in your backyard. I just heard a line in a Hallmark movie: "Traditions are the stories families write together. Keep writing your stories."

On a cold winter day, I told the residents at our Assisted Living Center, "The good news is that it is ninety degrees outside in Hawaii. The bad news is that it's ten below zero in Canton." I put a DVD on the screen featuring beaches and palm trees in Hawaii. All day long we greeted everyone with "Aloha" and wore bright multicolored Hawaiian leis. I gave everyone marshmallows and we had a snowball fight after our exercise routine. We drank pineapple juice and concluded the activity with prayer. Always invite God into the celebrations of life. He celebrates you. He knows where you are!

CHAPTER FORTY FOUR
THE PRESENCE OF GOD
July 13, 2023

What an awesome privilege to have a personal relationship with our Heavenly Father! God is always there, but we have to enter into His presence. It is in His presence that we access His peace, His joy, and His rest. It is in His presence that fear, worry, and the tension from pressure and stress fades away. For the next few minutes, I'm inviting you to join me into a place of serenity. Nothing is more important than God's presence.

Are you ready? Go to your quiet space away from all the turmoil of the outside world. Fill the area with soft, tranquil music. Leave the frustrations and close the door. Get comfortable and ready to relax. Picture being in your favorite place in the world. It may be sitting on the beach with your toes in the sand, hearing the roar of the waves and watching God paint the colors of the sunrise. It may be sitting in your rocking chair in that place you call home or in front of a candle or fireplace watching the rhythm of the flames and feeling the warmth of the heat. Be still. Enjoy the quietness for a moment. Count to ten…. Now turn the page.

Let's pray: "Father, we thank You for inviting us into Your rest. Thank You for Your refreshing. Thank You for allowing us to experience Your unconditional love; for peace that bypasses our understanding; for joy that invades our innermost being as we focus on Your goodness. We surrender our thoughts to You now. Teach us to hear Your voice whispering, "Be still, and know that I am God," Psalm 46:10. Thank You for Your promise that "He who dwells in the secret place of the Most High shall abide under the shadow of the Almighty," Psalm 91:1.

It only takes three minutes to de-clutter our mind. Sit up straight. Take a deep breath. Inhale through your nose and hold it for three seconds. Slowly exhale. Gradually let go of stress and allow your muscles to relax for a moment. Slowly count to three. Take another deep breath. Hold it... one, two, three. Exhale. One more time. Each time, feel yourself letting go...You are doing good!

Now, start with the muscles in your face. Raise your eyebrows and hold them in position for a few seconds. Slowly, let go. Smile, and hold that position. Did you know a smile sends a message telling your brain that everything is okay? Take a deep breath. Slowly let it go. Let yourself relax. You will probably find yourself yawning right now because gentle exercises cause your body to begin to rest. Gently, tighten the muscles in your neck. Now, hold that position and count to three. Exhale. Relax. Very slowly move your neck in each direction. Hold it each time... and let go.

Relax. Take a deep breath... Tighten your shoulder muscles and let go. Feel the weight of the world becoming as light as a feather. See the burdens you have been carrying lifted from your shoulders as you release them into your Heavenly Father's care. Tighten each muscle group from your head to the tips of your fingers and finally to your toes. Hold it. Now take a deep "breath in... two, three. Out... two, three." Feel the tension leaving as you inhale the very presence of the One who created the air you breathe. He breathed into the nostrils of the very first man, and he became a living soul. Relax in the presence of your Creator.

"Enter into His gates with thanksgiving and into His courts with praise," Psalm 100:4. There is a place we can go past the gates of praise into the Holy of Holies. In the serenity of these moments, we go beyond knowing "about" God, and into a personal relationship "with" Him. Spending some time in His presence takes your focus from the temporal into that which is eternal. Our closest friends are those with whom we choose to spend the greatest amount of our time. Developing an intimate relationship with God builds trust and reveals the essence of His nature and character. It is impossible to know Him and not worship Him.

In the busyness of your daily routine, when you feel tense, take a five minute break. Go back to your secret place. Picture yourself in the cradle of God's love on the computer screen saver of your mind. Listen to a worship song in your heart and hear the sounds of music coming from your innermost being. If you know the tune to the following stanzas, hum along with me..."*In the presence of Jehovah, God, Almighty, Prince of Peace... troubles vanish, hearts are mended, in the presence of the King.*" He is not "a" king. He is "The" King of Kings! Sing with me: "*Oh come let us adore Him...*"

Meditate on His goodness and give thanks. Prayer is two-way communication. You can talk to God about anything. Expect Him to answer. Surrender to Him your mind, will, and emotions. As you open your heart to receive, God will open your eyes to see what He sees, and ears to hear what He hears. Isaiah 40:31 says, "But those who wait upon the Lord, Shall renew their strength. They shall mount up with wings like eagles."... "In quietness and confidence shall be your strength," Psalm 8:1. His manifested presence not only surrounds you, but envelops your very being.

Last night at church at the end of the service my son asked everyone to close their eyes. He asked, "What do you see? Ask God to show you what He sees. Start visualizing the answers to your prayers. Ask God to show you the needs of others in your neighborhood, your community, or even someone on the other side of the globe. God may send you to a nursing home or hospital room, a neighbor or stranger. A Hallmark slogan is: "You can change the world, if you care."

Years ago, while my husband and I were grocery shopping, a couple who had visited our church asked Herschel to pray for a foster child they were hoping to adopt. The baby needed a miracle. They were shocked when he began praying for David out loud in the aisle. I watched the mother, with tears in her eyes place her trust in God for His perfect will.

Miracles happen on *"both"* sides of eternity. It was a Divine appointment. The couple became dear friends and members of our church. Mark later served in a leadership position at the Cathedral of Life for many years as an advisor and spiritual Elder until he stepped from time into eternity. David was waiting for him...

When you, or someone you know needs a miracle, Jesus said in Luke 11:9, "Ask, and it will be given to you; seek, and you will find; knock, and it will be opened to you." God is the supreme, sovereign, ultimate authority. Our faith is founded on trust. Make these declarations today: "I dare to believe! I also trust God's decisions. Miracles still happen!" He knows where you are.

"Yesterday is history.
Tomorrow is a mystery.
Today is a gift,
that's why we call it the present."
-Bill Keane

Unwrap the gift,
and expect surprises in each new day.

CHAPTER FORTY FIVE
THE EPILOGUE

I didn't realize that the pages of this book would become a journal taking me on a seventy five year journey down memory lane.

The reminders of the many miracles along the way continue giving me faith and courage to face the shocking changes that are taking place in my present. Today I had to choose a headstone that included my name. As I walked away, the feelings of dread disappeared. Herschel's departure date reminded me of the everlasting adventure God has planned for us in eternity.—He's there!

I didn't know when I wrote, *"The Miracle on 38th Street,"* that soon we would watch black smoke pour out of the windows of our church. I didn't realize it would be a year before the demolition and the renovation would finally begin. With the exception of the exterior walls and the Bibles that were placed in the foundation, everything in the interior, including the electrical wiring, will leave the building. Someday, it will be new again. The lights will be turned back on. To God be the glory!

Every time we moved our church congregation to another new location, we felt like the Israelites following the cloud by day and the fire by night during their exodus from Egypt. They had air conditioning from the heat of the sun and warmth for the cool of the night. Every need was supplied by God's *"Unlimited Provision."* When they entered into the promised land, they went from being the children of Israel to becoming the Nation of Israel. God always has a plan!

God uses the triumphs of the past to inspire our faith to face the future. God used *"The Spider"* to help me remember He has a plan for my life. He used *"The Sunflower, The Storm, The Surprise, The Lily of the Valley, The Earring, and The Wish"* to remind me that His GPS knows exactly where I am. His protection in *"The Angelic Encounters, The Eagle, and The Tornado"* was amazing.

I was reminded of the Divine destiny God has for each of us in *"The Rose, The Sign, and The Dream."* I experienced His faithfulness to keep His promises in *"The Lion, The Prom-ise Dress, and The Wedding."* I saw Him in *"The Design"* and heard the sound of His voice in *"The Challenge and The Wake Up Call."* I watched God perform miracles in *"every story."*

I didn't realize when I wrote the first chapter, that very soon my husband's journey would take him through *"The Last Mile"* beyond the stars into the eminent, manifested presence of God. Two days before the first anniversary of his home-going the memorial stone finally arrived. We decided to go together as a family to the burial garden. When we arrived, a white feather floated down and landed on the head stone.

Michael shared an amazing story. When he woke up that morning he said to God, "This is the day papa died." God spoke to him, "His birthdate is the day he was born into time. Today is the first anniversary of his birth into the eternal realm. Celebrate his forever birthday." Michael brought a cake and lit a candle. We sang, *"Happy Birthday."* As we stood at the burial garden in the shadow of the airport, we started singing the old song, *"When I die, hallelujah by and by, I'll fly away."* Our two year old, great-granddaughter, Isabella, kept shouting, "Sing it again!" As we sang, our tears turned into laughter. Heaven is a real place.

We went to dinner together and celebrated good times. I gave everyone a gold feather to remind them that although their earthly father is in "Heaven," their Heavenly Father is still here. I didn't realize that our 55th Wedding Anniversary would be our last. I don't know what lies ahead, but I know God is in *"The Times and Seasons."* He will be there in every storm, on the mountain or in the valley, providing a way in every desert. I trust Him with *"The Big Picture."*

He enlarged our vision in *"The Assignment"* to take His love to our world that is hurting. Just recently, six students from a local high school committed suicide. It was shocking. A young lady from our church asked friends on Facebook to join her to pray at a park near the school. Over 300 people came in freezing weather and 1700 more joined us via electronics from other locations.

I watched as the balloons and prayers went up into the atmosphere lifting the banner of hope into a broken-hearted community and declaring the diabolical powers of darkness powerless in their assignment over that region. While the lights are out in our church on 38th street, the Church of Jesus Christ is still alive and well. Churches from around the city united with us in prayer. His Holy presence invaded the atmosphere!

It has been a fascinating journey. Every mile has stories of answered prayers. I valued the guidance and instruction through His Holy Spirit in the *"The Abundant Life, The Gammill House, The Lost and Found Department, and The Stress Factor."* The love of God that was expressed in *"The Christmas Present and The Message"* was incredible. As we recognize and enjoy *"The Presence of God"* each day is filled with *"The Celebration of Life."* Through God's plan in *"The Restoration Process"* we have the ability of *"The Overcomer"* to face every trial in life with victory and triumph.

Life is lived one day at a time in a series of new beginnings and unexpected surprises. I just found out I have two great-grandsons, Issac and Levi arriving this summer. I can't tell you how excited I am. Life will continue and we will keep pursuing each new assignment and experiencing miracles in every season. Every new day will be filled with God's presence because He will never leave or forsake us... He promised!

One time when I was feeling distraught over a traumatic situation, I went to the mall to walk and pray. I noticed a parked police car on the parking lot. The patrolman was reading what looked like a Bible. Since it was hot outside and his windows were rolled down, I stopped and asked what he was reading. He began reading that same promise, "Lo, I am with you always... I will never leave you nor forsake you." I said, "Thank you." It took courage to ask but God arranges unusual ways to speak to me, and as always, God was there!

I hope that on the pages of this book you saw God as "your" loving Heavenly Father and know that He truly is "Beyond Awesome." I don't know the places your journey is taking you today, but I know His presence will show up unexpectedly like the rain on a hot summer day, or the gentle cool breeze in the hours before dawn, announcing:
"He Knows Where You Are."

"Be Strong
and of good courage;
do not be afraid, nor be dismayed,
for the Lord your God is with you
wherever you go."

-Joshua 1:9

ALPHABETIZED CONTENTS

The Abundant Life 169
The Angelic Encounters 157
The Answers... 221
The Assignment 135
The Big Picture 175
The Celebration of Life 251
The Challenge 35
The Christmas Present 57
The Cross and the Switchblade 83
The Design 19
The Divine Love Connection..................... 93
The Dream.. 29
The Eagle 165
The Elephant Earring 195
The Epilogue 265
The Gammill House 111
The Inn.. 117
The Introduction... 1
The July Fourth Weekend 67
The Last Mile 141

The Lily of the Valley	183
The Lion	43
The Lost and Found Department	201
The Message	79
The Miracle on 38th Street	105
The Overcomer	227
The Presence of God	259
The Prom-ise Dress	47
The Questions	215
The Red Dress	75
The Restoration Process	243
The Robin	123
The Rose	25
The Seed	207
The Sign	151
The Spider	61
The Storm	15
The Stress Factor	235
The Sunflower	11
The Surprise	71
The Times and Seasons	5
The Tornado	187
The Unlimited Provision	99
The Wake up Call	129
The Wedding	191
The Wish	53

MY PRAYER FOR YOU

I pray that this book will be anointed to unveil the greatness of our God. I pray that the struggles and victories I share from the journal of my life will inspire you to see the invisible, hear the inaudible, and experience the reality of God beyond your greatest expectation.

May you see life in its true perspective: to not fall in love with the things of time, but to love and cherish that which is eternal. May you live, not merely to exist, but fulfill the purpose for which you were created. May your faith be increased to believe God for the impossible and experience His miraculous intervention in your life.

May you celebrate God's presence, knowing that it is a gift and whatever each day brings, you will never be alone. May the stories on the pages of this book motivate you to discover God's GPS guiding your steps into unforgettable adventures of abundant living. May you "always" remember God loves you... and He knows where you are.
        In the name of the Father, the Son,
          and the Holy Spirit. Amen.

ABOUT THE AUTHOR

Gail Gammill was born and raised in the state of Kansas. At the age of four, she dedicated her life to Jesus Christ. As a teenager, she went to New York City and joined David Wilkerson's Teen Challenge street ministry to teen gangs and drug addicts. She was there during the time the book, *"The Cross and the Switchblade,"* was being written.

Following her ministry with Teen Challenge, Gail met her husband, Herschel, while attending Lee University in Cleveland, Tennessee. They were blessed with a precious son and daughter, three grandchildren on earth, two in Heaven, and four great-grandchildren. Their ministry took them to many continents and across the nation sharing the Gospel of Jesus Christ, building churches, and conducting evangelistic crusades They pioneered, founded, and pastored eight churches including the Cathedral of Life in Canton, Ohio.

Gail was very much involved in her husband's ministry, including the "Life in the Spirit" telecasts and speaking on his daily radio broadcasts. She founded the "Ladies of Life" women's ministries and conducted "Life" support groups and Bible studies. She was the featured speaker in many Children's Crusades, Youth Camps, and Women's Retreats and Conferences.

Gail was an integral part of the music ministry at the Cathedral as a soloist, organist, and directing dramas and musical presentations. She served in the Care Ministry visiting hospitals and nursing homes and was passionately involved in personal witnessing through Evangelism Explosion. She served as the Executive Director of the Cathedral Child Care Center and is now employed as the Chaplain at our Assisted Living Center, The Inn at Belden Village.

Gail's testimony and simple childlike faith in God inspires, strengthens, and builds the faith of those to whom she is given the opportunity to minister. Her greatest joy has always been the luxury of being allowed to have spiritual influence in the lives of her precious family.

Her greatest accomplishment was the privilege of helping raise up generations of young people who love God with all their heart. As each of them share the Gospel through their own worldwide endeavors, the Gammill family is continuing the Cathedral of Life Ministries in Canton, Ohio.

"The Lord bless you and keep you;
The Lord make His face
to shine upon you;
And be gracious to you;
The Lord lift up His countenance
upon you, and give you peace."
-Numbers 6:24

FOR INFORMATION

If you have a prayer request or
wish to order additional books you may
contact:

Gail Gammill
Cathedral of Life
4111 38th Street N.W.
Canton, Ohio 44718
330 493-5433 (Life)
or 330 493-4111
e-mail address:
info@cathedraloflife.org.

Jesus said,
"If two of you agree on earth
concerning anything that they ask,
it will be done for them by My Father in
heaven. For where two or three are gathered
together in My name
I am in the midst of them."
                                    -Matthew 18:19-20